DAY BY DAY
with
POPE JOHN PAUL II

DAY BY DAY
——— *with* ———
POPE JOHN PAUL II

reflections for each day of the year

edited by
Angelo Pisani

paulist press *new york/ramsey*

Book design by Theresa M. Sparacio

Library of Congress
Catalog Card Number: 82-81185

ISBN: 0-8091-2458-0

Published by Paulist Press
545 Island Road, Ramsey, N.J. 07446

Printed and bound in the
United States of America

CONTENTS

PREFACE

This book of short passages from the writings of Pope John Paul II, arranged for spiritual meditation on each day of the year, was first published in Italian under the title *Giorno per Giorno con Papa Wojtyla.* A shortened form of the original foreword by the publisher, Piero Gribaudi, follows the preface and will explain the purpose behind the choice of passages. The Paulist Press thought it worthy of translation for the English-speaking world because of the rich variety of reflections that are made available from the remarkable thoughts of this pope. It allows a reader to pray each day with the help of the spiritual insights of one man, Karol Wojtyla, who has been teacher, bishop and pope, but also has had to suffer and struggle and ponder in very difficult tasks of leadership. At the same time, this collection provides refreshingly new glimpses of the man in his prayers, some of which are very philosophical while others are almost lyrical in poetry and song.

Hopefully this book will be a prayer book, giving food for meditation and praise of God each day. It is not pretentious, nor does it claim to present the thoughts of John Paul II systematically or completely, nor even to have gathered the best, or the latest, or the most profound of his words. In this sense, it is similar to an earlier book published by the Paulist Press, *Words of Certitude,* also translated from the Italian, which offered excerpts from the Pope's speeches on the theme of human hopefulness and the search for God. As in that volume, we have added several new passages to the English edition, especially in places where the original Polish poem could not be rendered well into Italian and then into English. We thought it better to include some of the thoughts and reflections from the more recent papal trips to Brazil and Germany and the United States in order to broaden the choice for the reader. The full list of new additions will be found in the bibliographical note at the end of the volume.

I am grateful to Mr. Anthony Buono for his patient and careful attention to the translation of this volume. He always gives more to the choice and exactness of expression than is demanded. The additional selections are due to his insight and judgment. A word of thanks must also go to Joe Isola, the dedicated copy editor of the Paulist Press who has given much time and energy to making sure the text flows smoothly and avoids language that seems foreign to the Spartan usage of American English. This is particularly true of the frequent use of "Man" in the original when speaking of the whole human race. In order to be sensitive to current concern with excessively masculine language, we have occasionally used other terms in expressing the same thought. But because this usage is so much a part of the style of the Pope's original philosophical way of speaking, we did not categorically eliminate all cases for fear that we would rob his words of their power and directness.

Lawrence Boadt, C.S.P.
Editor

FOREWORD TO THE ORIGINAL EDITION

In order to be reborn there is only one remedy: to rediscover the symbol of the day, especially in the image of the daily course of the sun, the simplest metaphor of human existence in its rising, manifestation, decline and setting: to take hold of the day with that fear and trembling with which life is grasped in its most beautiful moments, and to make every day a life.

Indeed, to live day by day gives us anew the wisdom that disappears when we hold only the large perspective; it forces us to know what we are doing, to give a meaning to everything, whether "useful" or "useless," to speak in terms of hours and minutes, to rediscover the pulse of time as of a heart that encloses and nourishes us.

However, some type of link is needed if we are to graft one day on another, to make every day not merely a splintered fragment but a stone that in union with another stone builds up a dwelling that is livable and well inserted into the human landscape. For some, this link will be prayer, for others a pause for "recollection," and for still others a brief and incisive reading.

The present volume has been conceived and put together with this last view in mind. We have chosen Pope John Paul II as the inspiration for our journey, not because he is "relevant" but because of three precise reasons. Pope John Paul II speaks authoritatively, articulates clearly, and talks simply.

Authoritativeness—which signifies strong assumption of responsibility, wisdom lived and not dreamed, ardor of convictions as a result of ardor of ideas—is colored in Karol Wojtyla by a nuanced originality: it becomes an authentic "spiritual fatherhood."

It is that readiness, or rather that willingness, to involve himself in all the dramas of his sons and daughters that is the generative gesture par excellence.

Whoever reads the passages in this book will experience this immediately. These passages leave their mark not because of their profundity of doctrine but above all because of that authoritative experience that comes through them and that more than only the words has a captivating effect as example. What in fact is authoritativeness if not an example that stimulates, comforts, and encourages? Example that does not impose itself but causes us to grow within ourselves?

The clarity of John Paul II does not become a lamp just for our parlor but a light by which to lay bare our ambiguities and make us come out of our hiding places. To applaud this clarity can be the most convenient means not to let ourselves be penetrated by it through and through. It will be noted, therefore, that several of the passages that are seemingly "comforting" are in reality tremendously demanding of us, not of "others."

Finally, there is "simplicity," which according to the adage is the most difficult thing in the world. Pope John Paul's simplicity, beyond the cordiality of the speech (which is something very different) is that of the Gospel: terribly demanding. After the ideological ponderings of the last few years, which are presently demonstrating all their obscene impotence, the time has come for incisive and fruitful simplicity. However, we must cling to it completely and intimately, far removed from every childish action and from every domestic spiritualism. Simplicity is disarming in its strength, synthesis and concentration.

It is to this concrete, effective, operative, daily day-by-day simplicity that Pope John Paul's directness calls us.

And the passages in this book call us anew to such a daily commitment, substantiated by work and sweat.

The evangelical "why worry about tomorrow . . .?" is certainly not the invitation to evasion. It is a sober and definitive call to live today and to die to it.

Piero Gribaudi

January

Truth Brings People Together

There is no peace without openness to sincere and continuous dialogue.

Truth itself is fashioned in dialogue, and it reinforces this indispensable instrument of peace.

Neither does truth fear honest agreements, because truth confers those insights that enable you to commit yourselves to it without sacrificing essential convictions and values.

Truth brings people together. It reveals what already unites the parties, first with one another. It causes yesterday's differences to recede and prepares the ground for new progress in justice and brotherhood, in the peaceful cohabitation of all people.

Challenge of God

Epiphany is the great feast of faith. Participants in this feast are both those who have already arrived at faith and those who are on the path toward it. They participate in it by giving thanks for the gift of faith, just as the Magi Kings, filled with gratitude, knelt before the Child.

The Church also participates in this feast—the Church,

who each year becomes more aware of the enormity of her mission. To how many people she must still bring the faith!

How many people must be led once more to the faith that they have lost, and this is at times more difficult than the first conversion to faith.

However, the Church—aware of this great gift, the gift of the incarnation of God—can never stop, never become weary. She must continually seek access to Bethlehem for every era. Epiphany is the feast of the challenge of God.

A Man Is Measured by the "Heart"

What measure shall we use to measure a man? Shall we measure him with the measure of the physical forces at his disposal? Or shall we measure him by the senses that allow him contact with the external world? Or again, shall we measure him with the measure of the intelligence that is verified by various tests or examinations?

We must measure people with the measure of the "heart."

In biblical terminology, the heart signifies our spiritual interiority; in particular, it signifies conscience. . . . Hence, we must measure people with the measure of conscience, with the measure of the spirit opened out to God. Only the Holy Spirit can fill this heart, that is, lead it to self-fulfillment by means of love and wisdom.

Our Eternity Passes Through Love

Love is not a risk. It gets its flavor from the whole person. It has its specific weight—the weight of one's whole destiny. It cannot perdure for only a moment. Our eternity passes through love. This is why it is found in the dimension of God—he alone is Eternity.

Love God in Order to Love Others

Persons who have loved God without reserve are particularly capable of loving others and of giving themselves to them without personal interests and without limits.

An Existence and a Love at Our Disposal

Sometimes human life seems to be too short for love. At other times it is human love that seems to be too brief for a long life. Or possibly too superficial.

In any case, we have at our disposal an existence and a love: how are we to fashion these into a unit that will make sense?

Then this unit can never be closed in on itself. It must be open because, on the one hand, it must influence other beings and, on the other hand, it must always reflect absolute Being and Love. It must reflect them at least in some way.

Hands Are the Landscape of the Heart

Hands are the landscape of the heart.
Hands often split

like ravines in the mountains, wherein an undefined
    force rolls.
Those hands that man opens only
when they have had their fill of work—
and then sees that, thanks to him alone,
others can walk in peace.

Hands are a landscape.
When they split, in sores,
pain arises and flows freely, in waves.
Yet man does not think of the pain.
No, with such pain coincides greatness:
the greatness of man, whose exact definition he
    himself does not know.

The Rights of God

The more we are aware of God's love toward us, the
more we understand the rights that God possesses over our
person and our love.

True Love and the Grace of God Would Never Allow Marriage to Become a Self-Centered Relationship

Married people must believe in the power of the Sacrament to make them holy; they must believe in their vocation to witness through their marriage the power of Christ's
love.
    True love and the grace of God would never allow
marriage to become a self-centered relationship of two individuals, living side by side for their own interests.

The "Chances" for Tomorrow

Love determines the future.

Prayer Animates the World

The conquest of the inner areas offers God the right place in the human spirit, that whole commitment that we could equate with the primacy of the "Pray" aspect. It is not absolutely in opposition with but rather grants respite and gives creative intuition to true openness—to the social sphere, the daily duty borne, and the living forces of work and culture, thus animating the great and arduous world of "Work" with fervent exhilaration and a spirit of service.

Prayer Gives Meaning to All of Life

Prayer is the first expression of man's interior truth.
The first condition of the authentic freedom of the spirt.
Prayer gives meaning to all of life in its every moment and in its every circumstance.

Prayer and Work

Prayer, which in every human work produces the reference to God the Creator and Redeemer, contributes to the total humanization of work.

"Work exists until we rise" (C. K. Norwich).

Man, who by the will of the Creator has been called from the beginning to subdue the earth by work, has been created likewise in the image and likeness of God himself. He cannot find himself in any other way or confirm who he is except by seeking God in prayer. In seeking God and encountering him in prayer, man must necessarily find himself again, since he is like God. He cannot find himself in any other way except in his prototype.

He cannot confirm his "dominion" over the earth except by praying contemporaneously.

JANUARY 14

It Is the Interior Work That Forms Man

The living contact with the Lord Jesus—the contact of a disciple with the Master—initiates and develops man's most sublime activity: the work on himself that has as its goal the formation of his humanity.

In our life, we prepare ourselves to carry out various works in one or another profession; interior work, on the other hand, tends uniquely to form man himself: that man who is each one of us. This work is the most personal collaboration with Jesus Christ, similar to the collaboration that was verified in his disciples when he called them to intimacy with himself.

JANUARY 15

The Austere Commitment of Holiness

The commitment of holiness entails austerity of life, serious control of one's desires and choices, a constant commitment to prayer, and an attitude of obedience and docility to the directives of the Church, both in the doctrinal, moral, or pedagogical sphere and in the liturgical sphere.

Build on the Foundation That Is Christ

Christ calls you, but he calls you in truth. His call is demanding, because he invites you to let yourselves be completely "captured" by him, so that your whole lives will be seen in a different light. He is the Son of God, who reveals to you the loving face of the Father. He is the Teacher, the only one whose teaching does not pass away, the only one who teaches with authority. He is the friend who said to his disciples: "No longer do I call you servants . . . but I have called you friends" (Jn 15:15). And he proved his friendship by laying down his life for you.

His call is demanding, for he taught us what it means to be truly human. Without heeding the call of Jesus, it will not be possible to realize the fullness of your own humanity. You must build on the foundation that is Christ (1 Cor 3:11); only with him will your life be meaningful and worthwhile.

Non-Truth Is Violence and War

If it is certain—and no one doubts it—that truth serves the cause of peace, it is equally indisputable that "non-truth" goes hand in hand with the cause of violence and war.

By "non-truth" we must understand all forms and all levels of absence, refutation, and mockery of truth: falsehood in the strict sense, partial and deformed information, sectarian propaganda, manipulation of the means of communication, and the like.

There Is No Good Without Truth

The thought that creates the true good must bear in itself a sign of truth.

Human Life and Culture

Man lives a truly human life thanks to culture. Human life is culture in the sense that by its means man distinguishes and differentiates himself from all that exists in the visible world. Culture is a way of being and existing on the part of man.

The Greatness of Knowing How to Learn

Great is the man who is always disposed to learn, whereas the one who thinks he already knows everything is in reality filled with self and hence devoid of the sublime values that truly enrich life.

Common Witness to the Faith

The quest for unity—whether through dialogue or through collaboration wherever possible—has as its goal the witness to be rendered to Christ today. This common witness is limited and incomplete so long as we are in disagreement concerning the content of the faith that we must proclaim.

This accounts for the importance of unity for today's evangelization. Christians must be eager to bear witness together to the gifts of faith and life received from God. However, the problem is not solely that this witness must be common but that it must be an authentic witness of the Gospel, a witness borne to Christ in the fullness of his Church.

In this sense, it is necessary for Christians—and I think especially Catholics—to deepen their fidelity to Christ and to his Church.

United Witness to Christ

Jesus calls us to bear witness to himself and his salvific work. We can do so adequately only when we shall be completely united in faith and when we shall pronounce his word with a single voice, a voice that resounds with the warm vitality that characterizes the whole Christian community when it lives together in full communion.

Our divisions hinder this vitality and impede our neighbors from hearing the Gospel as they should. And yet, even now, thanks to all that we already have in common, it is possible for us, in spite of these divisions, to render a sincere though limited witness together to the world. This world has so much need of hearing that message of love and hope that is the good news of salvation gained by Christ for the whole human race.

Evangelization Awaits "Signs of Unity"

In the course of almost a millennium, the two sister Churches, the Catholic and the Orthodox, flourished side by side like two great, vital, and complementary traditions of the same Church of Christ. They maintained not only peaceful and fruitful relations but also the help of the indispensable communion in faith, in prayer, and in love, which at no cost were they willing to subject to dispute in spite of their different sensitivities.

The second millennium, on the contrary, has been darkened—except for a few fleeting rays of sunshine—by the distance that the two Churches have mutually placed between them, with all the distressing consequences. The wound is not yet healed.

But the Lord can heal it, and he enjoins us to do the best we can. We are now at the end of the second millennium. Is it not time to hasten the pace toward perfect fraternal reconciliation, so that the dawn of the third millennium will find us once again side by side, in full communion, bearing common witness of salvation to the world?

The Unity of Christians, Captivating Duty of Our Time

I regard the effort to bring about the unity of Christians as one of the most sublime and captivating duties of the Church in our time. You would like to know if I expect this unity and how I imagine it. I will give you the same reply that I have given you concerning the realization of the Council.

Here, too, I see a particular calling of the Holy Spirit. Insofar as the realization [of unity] is concerned, and the various stages of that realization, we find all of the basic elements in the teaching of the Council.

We must bring about these elements, seek to apply them concretely, and above all always pray with fervor, constancy, and humility. The unity of Christians can be realized only by a profound maturation in truth and a continual conversion of hearts.

When God Addresses His Word to Us He Communicates Himself

When God communicates his Word to us, he does not give us any information about things or other persons; he does not communicate "something" to us, but he communicates himself.

As the excellent strong Word of God's conveying of himself to us, Jesus is God himself at the same time. Thus, God's Word requires an answer, and this answering word is to be given with the whole of our person.

To Proceed Is to Be Aware of the End

Every man proceeds—toward the future. Nations also proceed. So does all humanity. To proceed means not only to undergo the exigencies of time, continuously leaving the past behind: yesterday, the years, the centuries. . . . To proceed means also to be aware of the end.

Can it be that man and the human race in their journey on this earth merely pass through it and disappear? Does man's entire existence consist in what he builds, achieves, and enjoys on this earth? Independently of all the achievements and the whole of life (culture, civilization, technology), does nothing else await him? "The figure of this world is passing away!" And does man pass completely away with it?

The words that Christ pronounces at the moment of his taking leave of the apostles express the mystery of the history of man—of each one and of all—the mystery of the history of mankind.

When God Calls Us He Desires All of Our Vital Energies

We should dwell frequently on the fact that God, when he calls us, does not ask us for only a part of our person. He asks for our whole person and all of our vital energies, to proclaim to all men the joy and peace of the new life in Christ, to lead them to the encounter with him.

Our first concern must be to seek the Lord and, once we have encountered him, to ascertain where and how he lives, and to remain with him the whole day (Jn 1:39). We must remain with him in a special way in the Eucharist, where Christ gives himself to all of us, and in prayer, through which we give ourselves to him. The Eucharist must be completed and prolonged in our daily affairs like "a sacrifice of praise" (Roman Missal).

In prayer, in faithful dialogue with God our Father, we discern better wherein lies our strength and wherein lies our weakness, because the Spirit comes to our assistance (Rom 8:26).

The same Spirit speaks to us and immerses us little by little in the divine mysteries, the designs of love for men, which God carries out through our readiness to serve him.

To Exclude Christ from the History of Man Is an Action Against Man

Without Christ, we cannot comprehend man in his fullness. Or rather, without Christ, man is incapable of comprehending himself in his fullness. He can neither understand who he is nor what his true dignity is, nor what his vocation is, nor what his ultimate destiny is. Without Christ, he cannot understand all of this. That is why we cannot exclude Christ from the history of man in any part of the globe nor in any geographical longitude or latitude.

The exclusion of Christ from man's history is an action against man.

Strong with the Power of Faith, Hope, and Love

You must be strong.

You must be strong with that power that comes from faith! You must be strong with the power of faith! You must be faithful! Today more than in any other age you need this power.

You must be strong with the power of hope that brings the perfect joy of living and does not sadden the Holy Spirit anew!

You must be strong with the power of love, which is stronger than death. You must be strong with that love that "is patient, is kind . . . is not envious . . . does not put on airs, is not snobbish, is not rude, is not self-seeking, does not brood over injuries, does not rejoice over injustice but rejoices in the truth. That love that will never end believes all things, hopes all things, and bears all things" (1 Cor 13:4–8).

You must be strong with the power of faith, hope, and love that is knowledgeable, mature, and responsible, and helps us to establish the great dialogue with man and with the world in this stage of our history. This dialogue with man and with the world is rooted in the dialogue with God himself—with the Father through the Son in the Holy Spirit—a dialogue of salvation.

Wherever Anyone Suffers There Christ Is Waiting

The Church, in looking at the mystery of the Son of God made man—and himself exposed through the injustice of men to suffering and hunger, to poverty, and to exile—cannot exempt herself from intervening, making a commitment, and becoming involved in order to assist men, and to save them from suffering.

Wherever anyone suffers, there Christ waits in his stead (Mt 25:31–46). Wherever anyone suffers, there the Church must be at his or her side.

Through Christ We Know God Above All in His Relationship of Love for Man

Although God "dwells in unapproachable light" (1 Tm 6:16), he speaks to man by means of the whole of the universe: "Ever since the creation of the world, his invisible nature, namely, his eternal power and deity, has been clearly perceived in the things that have been made" (Rom 1:20). This indirect and imperfect knowledge, achieved by the intellect seeking God by means of creatures through the visible world, falls short of a "vision of the Father."

"No one has ever seen God," writes St. John in order to stress the truth that "the only Son, who is in the bosom of the Father, he has made him known" (Jn 1:18). This "making known" reveals God in the most profound mystery of his being, one and three, surrounded by "unapproachable light" (1 Tm 6:16).

Nevertheless, through this "making known" by Christ we know God above all in his relationship of love for man: in his "philanthropy" (Ti 3:4). It is precisely here that "his invisible nature" becomes in a special way "visible," incomparably more visible than through all the other "things that have been made": it becomes visible in Christ and through Christ, through his actions and his words, and finally through his death on the cross and his resurrection.

(Original in *English Edition* of Encyclical *Rich in Mercy*, no. 2)

† † †

February

The Word of God, Foundation of a Complete Certitude

Divine in its substance although made up of human words, Scripture is infinitely authoritative: source of faith, according to the word of Paul, it is the foundation of a complete, undoubting, and unwavering certitude. Since all of it is from God, it is all, in its most minute part, infinitely important and worthy of the greatest attention.

Confronting the Word of God as Children

It is vitally necessary that the relationship with the Word of God be always worshipful, faithful, and loving.

In her proclamation, the Church must draw essentially from this Word, letting herself be guided by the very words of her Lord so as not to risk "reducing the words of religion to human words." Likewise, every Christian must refer to Scripture "always and everywhere" in all his choices, becoming "like a child" in its presence, and seeking therein the most effective remedy for all his diverse infirmities, and not daring to take one step without being enlightened by the divine rays of those words.

We Cannot Separate the Cross from Human Work

Whether it is the old type of work in the fields that yields fruit but thorns and thistles as well or the new type of work in blast furnaces and foundries, it is always accomplished through the "sweat of one's brow."

The law of the cross is inscribed in human work. By the sweat of his brow the iron industry worker toils. And by the sweat of his brow, by the tremendous sweat of death, Christ agonizes on the cross.

We cannot separate the cross from human work. We cannot separate Christ from human work.

Man's Worth Does Not Consist Solely in What He Produces

Remember this ancient fact: Christ will never approve that man be regarded—or even regard himself—solely as a means of production, that he be appraised, esteemed, and valued according to such a principle. Christ will never endorse this view! That is why he let himself be affixed to the cross, as on the great threshold of man's spiritual history, to oppose every degradation of man, even degradation by means of work.

Christ remains before our eyes on his cross, so that every man may be conscious of that power Christ has given him: "He has given them the power to become children of God" (Jn 1:12).

This fact must be kept in mind by the worker as well as the giver of work, by the system of work as well as the system of remuneration; it must be kept in mind by the state, the nation, and the Church.

Man's Task: To Be Vigilant

The accusation is frequently leveled at Christianity that, by directing man to ultimate and eternal realities, it diverts his attention from temporal things.

Such a reproach entails an erroneous understanding of Christ's summons to "be vigilant." This summons is pronounced in an eschatological perspective, but at the same time it is open to all the fullness of problems and tasks of the man who lives on earth.

Temporal existence generates a series of duties, which constitute precisely the content of that "be vigilant" according to the Gospel.

Work—An Impulse Toward Resurrection

The beautiful is necessary for man, and it is given to him by God under various aspects to attract man, whose vocation is to work.

Work that is imbued with the beautiful gives man an impulse toward the heights, toward resurrection. Without this impulse one cannot live; it is human, and at the same time it is profoundly Christian.

Materialism—Enslavement of Man to Man

If atheism in all of its forms is to be rejected, this is because of the truth of man, because it is always a cause of

enslavement for him. It is a case of enslavement to a soul-
less quest for material goods; it is a case of an even worse
enslavement of man, body and soul, to the atheistic ideologies. It is always in the end the enslavement of man to man.

That is why the Catholic Church has willed to recognize and solemnly proclaim the right to religious freedom in
the loyal quest for spiritual and religious values; that is
why, too, she prays that all men may find the path of total
truth in fidelity to the religious meaning that God has
placed in their hearts.

Every Innocent Human Life Is Sacred

There is the impression nowadays of the prevalence of
economy over morality, of the prevalence of the temporal
over the spiritual.

On the one side, the almost exclusive orientation
toward the consumerism of material goods deprives human
life of its deepest meaning. On the other side, work is becoming in many cases an alienating obligation for man,
subjected to collectives, and it is ever more detached from
prayer, depriving human life of its ultratemporal dimension.

Among the negative consequences of such a preclusion
of transcendent values, there is one that concerns us in a
special way nowadays. It consists in the ever more diffuse
climate of social tension, which so frequently degenerates
into absurd episodes of fierce terroristic violence. Public
opinion is profoundly shaken and disturbed by it.

Only the regained awareness of the transcendent dimension of human destiny can inculcate the obligation for
justice and the respect for the sacredness of every innocent
human life.

We cannot live for the future without intuiting that

the meaning of life is greater than temporality and is above it. If the societies and the men of our continent have lost interest in such a meaning, they must rediscover it.

Each of Us Has His Own Part in the History of the World

The destruction, or better the self-destruction, of this world, whose peril accompanies the consciousness of contemporary man, is delineated at the same time as a consequence of the prevalence of hatred over love and justice, that is, of evil over good, in the moral sense.

In this context, Christ's "be vigilant" takes on a particular clarity. It becomes a great human imperative, with international and universal dimensions.

We experience a profound duty to act in the spirit of this imperative, ceaselessly repeating the call to justice and peace in today's world.

True Science Must Be Inspired by Courage, Conscience, and Love

Science, in the phase of its concrete realizations, is necessary to humanity in order to satisfy the just demands of life and overcome the various evils that threaten it.

There is no doubt that applied science has brought and will bring immense services to man, as long as it is inspired by love, regulated by wisdom, and accompanied by courage that defends it from undue interference on the part of every tyrannical power.

Applied science must ally itself with conscience, so

that in the trinomial science-technology-conscience the cause of man's true good will be served.

The New Man Is Born of Faith

The most subtle temptation that nowadays afflicts Christians and especially the young is the temptation to renounce the hope in the triumphant affirmation of Christ.

The instigator of all malice, the Evil One, is ever strongly dedicated to snuffing out in everyone's heart the light of such a hope.

The path of a devout Christian is not an easy one, but we must traverse it in the awareness of possessing an inner power of transformation, communicated to us with the divine life that has been given us in Christ the Lord.

In virtue of your witness, you will show that the most sublime human values are assumed in a Christianity lived with coherence, and that the evangelical faith not only sets forth a new vision of man and the universe, but also provides the capability to bring about such a renewal.

Solidarity with Man, Solidarity with Christ

There is need for solidarity with each man without exception, especially with whoever has need of it: solidarity with one's own humanity when such humanity is in danger or is threatened.

Christ has taught us this solidarity, declaring that when we are united with everyone whose humanity is in the greatest danger we are united with Christ himself.

Mary—First Handmaid of the Eucharist

Mary is the first handmaid of the Eucharist, because in her the Word became flesh, and this is the same flesh that we receive, which is the food of our soul in view of time and eternity.

The Whole Life of Christ Was One Continuous Instruction

The majesty of Christ the teacher and the unique persuasive power of his teaching are explained solely by the fact that his words, parables, and teachings can never be separated from his life and his very being.

In this sense, Christ's whole life was one continuous instruction. His silences, his miracles, his actions, his prayer, his love for man, his predilection for the lowly and the poor, his acceptance of the supreme sacrifice on the cross for the world's redemption, and his resurrection are the actuation of his Word and the fulfillment of his revelation.

Man and His Struggles Are the Center of Catechesis

It is important to set forth without any hesitation the material demands of renunciation but also those of joy connected with what the apostle Paul loved to define as "new life," "new creation," "to be (or to exist) in Christ," and "eternal life in Jesus Christ." This is really nothing more than life in the world, but a life in accord with the beatitudes and a life called to project itself and transform itself in the beyond.

It highlights the importance in catechesis of personal moral demands corresponding to the Gospel, of Christian attitudes in the face of life and the world—whether these be heroic or very simple. We call them Christian virtues or evangelical virtues.

It also highlights the concern that catechesis will have, wherever possible, not to omit but rather to clarify—in the act of giving instruction in faith—a few realities, such as man's action for his integral liberation, the search for a more united and fraternal society, and the struggles for justice and the building up of peace.

Man Is Poor But Not Because He Possesses Nothing

Man is poor, not because he possesses nothing but because he is bound—and especially when he is bound spasmodically and completely—to what he possesses. Such is the case when he is bound in a way as to be incapable of giving anything of himself, when he is incapable of opening out to others and giving himself to them.

Be Firm in Faith!

The Christian faith, that gift of the divine benevolence, must be preserved, protected, loved, and defended!

Be firm in faith! Faith spans for us the infinite spaces of transcendence, makes us bow our heads before God, unites us intimately with Jesus Christ, true God and true man, and opens our eyes to hope and to joy. Faith enables us to love others as brothers and sisters, because it works through charity (Gal 5:6), gives us the key to understanding the authentically revolutionary value of the evangelical beatitudes, and makes us the people of God!

This is faith in God, Creator and Father; faith in Christ, unique Savior and true Liberator; and faith in the Church, mother and teacher of truth.

In the midst of the continuous and periodic crises of human ideologies, let your faith and your hope be fixed on God (1 Pt 1:21).

FEBRUARY 18

At the Profound Sources of Truth

Building up peace is the concern of all men and all peoples. Indeed, since all have been endowed with hearts and minds and made in God's image, they are capable of making a genuine and sincere effort to maintain peace.

I invite Christians to this common effort so that they may provide the specific contribution of the Gospel, which leads to the profound sources of truth, that is, to the incarnate Word of God.

FEBRUARY 19

Jesus Is a Living Person

Love Jesus!
Jesus is not an idea, a feeling, or a memory!
Jesus is a "person" always living and present with us.

Life Is Beautiful and Grand Only Insofar as It Is Given

Life is intrepid and courageous: Jesus is still unknown by three quarters of mankind! Therefore, the Church has need of so many volunteer men and women missionaries to proclaim the Gospel! Stupendous ideals of charity and generosity, as well as dedication, stand before you and invite you! Life is beautiful and grand only insofar as it is given! Be intrepid! The supreme joy lies in love without pretense, in a pure giving of charity to one's brothers and sisters!

Love is docile and confident in the action of "grace." It is the Holy Spirit who penetrates souls and transforms peoples. The difficulties are ever immense, and especially today the faithful themselves, caught up in concrete history, are tempted by atheism, secularism, and moral autonomy. Hence, there is need of an absolute confidence in the work of the Holy Spirit (*Evangelii Nuntiandi*, no. 75). Therefore, the Christian is patient and joyous in his missionary work, even if he must sow in tears, accepting the cross and preserving the spirit of the beatitudes.

Love is industrious and constant, exercising itself in various types of missionary apostolates: example, prayer, suffering, and charity.

The Eucharist—Call to Conversion

The Eucharist is a great call to conversion. We know that it is an invitation to the banquet; that, by nourishing ourselves on the Eucharist, we receive in it the Body and Blood of Christ, under the appearance of bread and wine.

Precisely because of this invitation, the Eucharist is and remains the call to conversion. If we receive it as such a call, such an invitation, it brings forth in us its proper fruits. It transforms our lives. It makes us a "new man," a "new creature" (cf. Gal 6:15; Eph 2:15; 2 Cor 5:17). It helps us not to be "overcome by evil, but to overcome evil by good" (Rom 12:21). The Eucharist helps love to triumph in us—love over hate, zeal over indifference.

The call to conversion in the Eucharist unites the Eucharist with that other great sacrament of God's love, which is Penance. Every time we receive the sacrament of Penance or Reconciliation, we receive the forgiveness of Christ, and we know that this forgiveness comes to us through the merits of his death—the very death we celebrate in the Eucharist. In the Sacrament of Reconciliation we are all invited to encounter Christ personally in this way, and to do so frequently.

The Redemption Is Effected Concretely through the Cross

Man created by God and elevated by him to the sublime dignity of sonship bears within himself an irrepressible desire for happiness and experiences a natural aversion to every kind of suffering.

Jesus, on the other hand, in his work of evangelization—although he stooped down to the sick and suffering to heal and comfort them—did not suppress suffering itself. He willed to submit himself to all possible human suffering, both physical and moral, in his passion unto the mortal agony of Gethsemane (Mk 14:23), unto abandonment on the part of his Father on Calvary (Mt 27:46), unto the protracted agony and the death on the cross. Accordingly, he characterized as blessed those who are afflicted (Mt 5:4) and those who hunger and thirst for justice.

The redemption is effected concretely through the cross!

This attitude of Jesus reveals a profound mystery of justice and mercy, which involves us all in it, and through which every man is called to share in the redemption.

The Supreme Consolation

There are many and beautiful consolations in life, and progress has increased and perfected them. We must know how to evaluate and enjoy them in a just and holy way.

But the supreme consolation is and must still and always be the presence of Jesus in our life.

Jesus the Divine Redeemer has entered human history; he has placed himself by our side to walk with us in every path of life, to gather up our confidences, to enlighten our thoughts, to purify our desires, and to comfort our sorrows.

The Eucharist Is the Meeting Place of Heaven and Earth

Christian life unfolds daily in the exercise of the various professions and in human toil generally. . . . The Church waits with open arms for men and women engaged in building the earthly city and relies greatly on them for the building of a world "cut to human measure" . . . and to love God.

The liturgical life is the privileged place where this exchange between God and the human person takes place. The altar of the Eucharist, on which Jesus Christ, the true and eternal priest, offers himself in sacrifice to the Father

for the human race, is the meeting place of heaven and
earth.

We Must See the Good in Modern Society As Well As Its Shortcomings and Dangers

Despite the many prophets of doom, there is a great
amount of good in the world that we owe to new technical
achievements. The fact that in broad areas they contribute
to improving the living conditions of every individual and
of mankind as a whole is cause for joy and gratitude to
God, who is the Lord of our time.

In keeping with her mission of salvation, the Church
promotes and supports as much as she can whatever contributes to the enhancement and overall development of
man, as is clearly illustrated by the cooperative partnership
based on trust between state and Church in different areas
and at different levels.

However, this acknowledgment of what is good and
worthy of recognition in modern society should also help
us to see the shortcomings and dangers to which the people
of today are increasingly exposed. The brighter the light,
the more clearly defined are the shadows and the threatening darkness of undesirable developments.

Sing Always of Joy

Song is the most sublime language through which man
expresses his sentiments such as hope, expectation, love,
anguish, sorrow, and especially joy.

Sing always of joy! The joy of living, of being at peace with yourselves, with others, and with God!

The Christian Is a First Fruit of the Creatures of God

The Christian becomes convinced ever more each day of the enormous difficulty of his commitment. He must go against the current; he must bear witness to absolute but not visible truths; he must lose his earthly life in order to gain eternity; and he must make himself responsible even for his neighbor, to enlighten, edify, and save him.

But he knows he is not alone.

What Moses said to the Jewish people is immensely more true for the Christian people: "What great nation has the deity so close to it as the Lord, our God, is to us whenever we call upon him?" (Dt 4:7).

The Christian knows that Jesus Christ not only has become man to reveal the saving truth and redeem humanity but has also remained with us on this earth, mystically renewing the sacrifice of the cross by means of the Eucharist and becoming spiritual food for the soul and companion on the way of life.

This is who the Christian is: a first fruit of the creatures of God, who must keep his faith and his life pure and without stain.

Man, the Way of the Church

Does not Jesus say in the Gospel that he is "the way, the truth, and the life" (Jn 14:6)? Before truth and life, he characterizes himself as the way, that is, the authoritative way, the obligatory and simultaneously secure way for everyone who wishes to go to the Father and so attain salvation. It is certainly an image analogous to the one that presents Jesus as the light (Jn 8:12) or as the door (Jn 10:7).

At the basis of these images there is a substantially identical teaching: we must walk in the path traced by Jesus and illumined by Jesus. More simply, we must follow Jesus, who from the incarnation to Calvary has constantly sought out man and only man, to redeem him from sin and restore him to the divine life of grace.

Now the Church, if she is—as she must be under pain of losing her identity—the faithful continuator of the work of Jesus, must make provision to be herself the way for man. As already between Christ and the Church, so also between the Church and man there exists such a close relationship that one cannot stand without the other. This is why the reciprocal expression: man is the way of the Church, is correct and true; man constitutes the "primary and fundamental way" that the Church must traverse in fulfilling her mission.

The Body, Gift of Love

The body, which expresses femininity "through" masculinity and masculinity "through" femininity, manifests the reciprocity and communion of persons. It does so by means of the gift as a fundamental characteristic of personal existence. This is the body: it bears witness to creation as to a fundamental gift; hence, it bears witness to love as the fount from which this very giving has issued forth.

Masculinity-femininity—that is, sex—is the pristine sign of a creative giving, of an awareness on the part of man (male-female) of a gift lived so to speak in an original way. Such is the significance with which sex enters into the theology of the body.

† † †

March

The Tree of Life and the Liturgy of Death

"Remember that you are dust and into dust you shall return" (Gn 3:19). These are the words of the book of Genesis; in them we find the simplest expression of that "liturgy of death" in which man has become a participant as a consequence of sin.

The tree of life remained outside man's course when he went against God's will and proposed to assimilate the unknown reality of good and evil in order to become, in the fashion of the fallen angel, "like God" (Gn 3:15). And it was precisely then that man heard these words that have traced his destiny on earth.

Glory to You, O Christ, Word of God, in Every Place on Earth

Glory to you, O Christ, Word of God.

Glory to you every day of this blessed season that is Lent.

Glory to you, Word of God, who became flesh and manifested yourself with your life and accomplished your mission on earth with your death and resurrection.

Glory to you, Word of God, who penetrate the innermost part of human hearts, and show them the way of salvation.

Glory to you in every place on earth.

The Father's Response to His Children's Sin Is Called Mercy

Our reconciliation with God, our return to the house of the Father, is effected through Christ. His passion and death on the cross interpose themselves between every human conscience, every human sin, and the infinite love of the Father. Such love, quick to lift up and forgive, is nothing other than mercy.

Each of us, in personal conversion, in repentance, in the firm purpose of amendment, and finally in confession, agrees to accomplish a personal spiritual work, which is the prolongation and the distant reverberation of that saving work that our Redeemer has undertaken.

Here is how the Apostle expresses reconciliation with God: "God made him who did not know sin, to be sin for our sakes, so that through him we might become the very holiness of God" (2 Cor 5:21). Let us then undertake this effort of conversion through him, with him, and in him. If we do not undertake it, we are not worthy of the inheritance of the redemption.

The Triumph of Love Over Consciousness of Sin

Man must painfully rediscover what he has lost—what he has deprived himself of—by committing sin and living in sin, so that he may grow into taking the decisive step: "I will rise and go to my father" (Lk 15:18).

He must once again look upon the countenance of that Father on whom he has turned his back and with whom he has severed relations so as to be able to sin "freely" and to squander "freely" the gifts received. He must seek out the Father's countenance admitting—like the young man in the parable of the prodigal son—that he has lost the dignity of a son and does not deserve any welcome in the paternal home.

At the same time, he must ardently desire to return. The certainty of the goodness and love that pertain to the essence of God's fatherhood should bring about in him the triumph over consciousness of sin and personal unworthiness. Indeed, such certainty should show itself as the only way out—to be undertaken with courage and faith.

MARCH 5

Lent, Season of Light

Lent is the season of a special encounter with Christ, who does not cease to speak of himself:

"I am the light of the world; whoever follows me . . . will have the light of life" (Jn 8:12). Such was the case—a long time ago—in the days of the primitive catechumenate. And such is the case today—in the days of the "second catechumenate."

Lent represents that blessed season in which each of us can, in a particular way, pass through the zone of light. A powerful and intense light issues from the cenacle, from Gethsemane, from Calvary, and ultimately from the Sunday of the resurrection. We must pass through this zone of light so that we may rediscover life in ourselves.

Pain Is a Mysterious Treasure

Suffering is not sterile; it is not wailing lost in the desert wind, nor some blind and inexplicable cruelty. Indeed, the Gospel explains and interprets it: pain constitutes the direct participation in Christ's redemptive sacrifice and, as such, it has a precious function in the life of the Church.

It is a mysterious but real treasure for all the faithful—by means of that circulation of grace which Christ the head spreads throughout his mystical body, and which the members of this body exchange with one another.

Do Not Wait for a "Qualified" Mendicant in Order to Practice Your Charity

The call to repentance and conversion signifies a call to inner openness "toward others." Nothing in the history of the Church and in the history of man can substitute for this call. It is a call that has infinite destinations.

It is directed to every man, and it is directed to each for reasons proper to each. Hence, everyone must see himself in the two aspects of the destination of his call.

Christ demands that I be open to "others." But to which "other"? To the one who is here at this moment! I cannot put off this demand of Christ to an indefinite moment when a "qualified" mendicant will come and hold out his hand. I must be open to each man, ready to "give myself." To give myself with what? It is well known that sometimes with a single word we can also strike him painfully, injure him, wound him; we can even "kill him" morally.

Hence, we must welcome this call of Christ in those

ordinary daily life situations and contacts with others where each of us is always the one who can "give" to others and at the same time the one who knows how "to accept" what others can offer us.

Anticipating the Needs of One's Neighbor

Almsgiving and fasting as both a means of conversion and of Christian penance are closely connected with each other.

Fasting signifies a mastery over oneself; it signifies the discipline of being demanding toward oneself and of being ready to renounce things: not only food but also enjoyments and various pleasures.

And almsgiving—in the wider and essential meaning—signifies the readiness to share joys and sadnesses with others and to give to one's neighbor and any needy person in particular; to share not only material goods but also the gifts of the spirit.

It is precisely for this reason that we must be open to others, pay attention to their various needs, sufferings, and misfortunes, and seek—not only in our resources but above all in our hearts, in our way of behaving and acting—the means to anticipate their needs and bring solace to their sufferings and misfortunes.

The Cross of Jesus Makes Pain Fruitful

If it is true that human pain remains a great mystery, it nonetheless receives meaning and indeed fecundity from the cross of Jesus. In the Lord's eyes, the suffering of the just and the innocent is precious in a special way, more than the suffering of the sinner. The latter suffers only for himself, for self-expiation, whereas the innocent turns pain into a means of redemption for others.

This is the case with Christ who, according to the Letter to the Hebrews, "offered himself once for all in order to take away the sins of many" (Heb 9:28; cf. 10:10).

This, too, is why we are Christians—to be like him in glory and in sorrow.

Therefore, we repeat St. Paul's words, in the awareness of their profound truth: "Just as the sufferings of Christ flow over into our lives, so also through Christ our consolation overflows" (2 Cor 1:5).

Hands Ready for Great Tasks

Whoever passes through the great catechesis of the cross, whoever contemplates its mystery, cannot come away from the cross with empty hands. He must feel that he possesses hands ready for great tasks; that he possesses a heart ready for true love; that all of life is worthy to be lived freely; for his own liberation and that of his neighbor, his family, his children, and his country.

The Truth of the Cross Is a Truth of Love

The cross is not a dialectic. In the cross lies cannot be said. The cross tells the whole truth.

The truth that is proclaimed by the cross is a truth of love.

God loved—the Father loved. He has expressed his

love by sacrificing his Son. And the Son has become the expression of the Father's love and taken it to its very limits, because he has accepted the cross and on the cross he has remained with us.

God Is Man's Friend and Works in Man and for Man

In the work of culture God makes an alliance with man; he himself becomes a cultural worker for the development of man. "You are God's cultivation," St. Paul exclaims (1 Cor 3:9).

Have no fear. . . . Open the gates of your minds, of your society, of your cultural institutions to God's grace. He is man's friend and works in man and for man, so that man may grow in his humanity and in his divinity, in his being and in his reality over the world.

The Cross, Fulcrum for Service to Man

The cross is the power point to use as a lever for a service to man, so as to transmit to so many others the immense joy of being Christian.

The Words Which Exorcise Sin

"Father, I have sinned against you . . ." (Lk 15:18). During the season of Lent, the Church will dwell on these words with particular emotion, because this is the season in which she desires to be more deeply converted to Christ. Without the words, "Father, I have sinned," man cannot truly enter into the mystery of Christ's death and resurrection, in order to obtain the fruits of the redemption and grace.

These are key ideas. They demonstrate above all man's great inner openness to God: "Father, I have sinned against you." If it is true that sin in a certain sense closes man up to God, confession of sins on the contrary opens to man's conscience all the greatness and majesty of God, and above all his fatherhood.

Man remains closed in his relations with God as long as the words, "Father, I have sinned," are missing from his lips; and especially as long as they are missing from his conscience and his heart.

To be converted to God, to experience the inner power of his cross and his resurrection, and to experience the full truth of human existence in him, "in Christ," is possible only with the power of the words, "Father, I have sinned," and solely at the cost of those words.

MARCH 15

The Cross Transforms the Meaning of Suffering

The way of historical man, defiled by sin, in fact unfolds under the sign of Christ's cross. In the cross, God has transformed the meaning of suffering: what was once the fruit and testimony of sin has now become a participation in the redeeming atonement effected by Christ.

As such, it bears the forewarning of the definitive victory over sin and its consequences, through participation in the Savior's glorious resurrection.

The Cross, Obligatory Way to the Encounter with God

Christ exercised his function as mediator above all through the immolation of his life in the sacrifice of the cross, accepted in obedience to the Father. The cross remains the "obligatory" way to the encounter with God. It is a path on which the priest is the first person who must set out with courage. Is he not called to renew "in the person of Christ," in the eucharistic celebration, the sacrifice of the cross?

According to the beautiful expression of the African Augustine of Hippo, Christ on Calvary was "priest and sacrifice, and therefore priest insofar as sacrifice." The priest who, in the radical poverty of obedience to God, the Church, and his bishop, knows how to make his life a pure oblation to offer, in union with Christ, to the heavenly Father, will experience in his ministry the victorious power of the grace of Christ dead and risen.

Jesus Has Overcome the Tyranny of Deceit and Falsehood

On the day when Jesus was crucified, he said to Pilate: "This is why I have come into the world: to testify to the truth" (Jn 18:37). Jesus came not to do his own will but the will of his heavenly Father.

By his words, by his actions, and by his whole existence he testified to the truth. In Jesus, defeat was inflicted upon the tyranny of deceit and falsehood, the tyranny of lying and error, and the tyranny of sin. For Christ is the Word of the divine truth who promised: "If you remain faithful to my word you will truly be my disciples: you will know the truth and the truth will make you free" (Jn 8:31–32).

The Church has received from Christ the same mission: to cultivate deep love and respect for the truth and to amalgamate the intuitions of human knowledge and wisdom into faith: in everything to testify to the truth. In all ages and in all countries the Church carries out his mission, confident in the knowledge that since God is the supreme source of all truth; there can be no opposition between natural wisdom and the truths of faith.

MARCH 18

The Remembrance of Christ Prevents Us from Sinning

Only the Eucharist, the true memorial of Christ's paschal mystery, is capable of keeping alive in us the remembrance of his love.

It is the secret of the Church's vigilance: otherwise, without the divine efficacy of this continuous and most precious reminder, without the penetrating power of her spouse's gaze fixed on her, it would be very easy for the Church to forget, to become insensitive, and to be unfaithful.

Only the Eucharist, by the design and gift of God, can preserve in our hearts the "seal" of that remembrance of Christ which holds us tight and prevents us from sinning.

MARCH 19

The Cross—a Sign of New Times

A symbol of the faith, the cross is also the symbol of the suffering which leads to the glory of the passion that culminates in the resurrection.

48

The cross of the Christian is always a paschal cross. Every time we celebrate the mystery of the cross, we increase our certainty—in the light of the faith—that the time of sacrifice and renunciation can really be the beginning of new times, times of realization and fullness.

A Lived Faith, Foundation of Human Dignity

The faith in God professed in common by descendants of Abraham—Christians, Mohammedans, and Jews—when it is sincerely lived and applied to life is both a secure foundation of the dignity, fraternity, and liberty of men and the principle of right moral conduct and life in society.

The Word of God Does Not Pass Away

The Church always rereads the same Gospel—the Word of God that does not pass away—in the context of the human reality that changes.

To Love One's Neighbor Means Above All Not to Hurt Him

If we take account of the essential meaning that "almsgiving" has for our conversion to God and for our entire Christian life, we must avoid at all costs everything that falsifies the sense of almsgiving, mercy, and works of charity: everything that can deform their image in us.

In this sphere it is very important to cultivate inner

sensitivities toward the real needs of our neighbor, in order to know in what aspect we should help him, how to act so as not to hurt him, and how to behave so that what we give, what we bring to his life, may be an authentic gift, a gift that is not diminished by the often negative sense of the word "almsgiving."

The Wounded Christ Gives Comfort and Reassurance in Suffering

Suffering is a terribly concrete and at times even atrocious and searing reality. Physical, moral, and spiritual pains afflict the poor humanity of all times. We must be grateful to technology, medicine, social, and civil organizations that seek in every way to eliminate or at least alleviate suffering. But suffering remains ever victorious and defeat weighs heavily upon afflicted and powerless man. Indeed, it seems almost as if a greater social progress is always accompanied by a moral retrogression, leading to other sufferings, fears, and anxieties.

Suffering is also a mysterious and disconcerting reality.

Yet we Christians, by contemplating Jesus crucified, find the strength to accept this mystery. The Christian knows that, in the aftermath of the original sin, human history is always a risk. But he also knows that God himself has willed to enter into our pain, to experience our contortions, to endure the agony of the spirit and the torment of the body. Faith in Christ does not take away suffering but sheds light on, elevates, purifies, sublimates that suffering, and makes it valid for eternity.

In any moral or physical pain, let us look to the Crucified One. Let the Crucified One reign in your homes with full visibility and true devotion. He alone can comfort and reassure us.

The Ways of Conversion

Prayer, almsgiving, and fasting demand a profound understanding if we want to make them a real part of our life rather than considering them simply as passing practices that require only something momentary from us.

The latter way of thinking will prevent us from arriving at the true meaning and the real strength that prayer, fasting, and almsgiving possess in the process of conversion to God and toward our own spiritual maturity.

One goes hand in hand with the other: we mature spiritually by becoming converted to God, and conversion comes about through prayer, as well as through fasting and almsgiving, properly understood.

The Triumph of Hope Over Anguish and Death

Mary is ever the most complete fulfillment of the saving mystery—from the immaculate conception to the assumption—and she continually foreshadows that mystery.

She reveals salvation and brings grace even to those who seem to be the most indifferent and far removed.

In the world, which together with its progress manifests its "corruption" and its "aging," she never ceases to be—in the words of Paul VI—"the beginning of the better world." Among other things, the lamented Pontiff writes: "To contemporary man, the Blessed Virgin Mary . . . offers a serene vision and a reassuring word: the triumph of hope over anguish, communion over solitude, peace over disturbance, joy and beauty over tedium and nausea . . . life over death."

The Anxiety and Joy to Discover the Truth

Seeking Jesus personally with the anxiety and joy to discover the truth gives a deep inner satisfaction and a great spiritual strength to put into practice what the truth demands, even at the cost of sacrifice.

Suffering Knows No Limits

Human suffering is a continent whose limits none of us can say we have reached.

Sensitive to All Suffering and Human Misery

We must become particularly sensitive to all suffering and human misery, to all injustice and wrong, seeking the way to remedy them in an effective manner.

Let us learn to discover with respect the truth of the inner person, because this inner person becomes the dwelling of God present in the Eucharist. Christ comes into the hearts and visits the consciences of our brothers and sisters. The experience of the eucharistic mystery fills us with love for our neighbor and for every man.

The Nuptial Character of the Body

The human body with its sexuality, with its masculinity and femininity—seen in the very mystery of creation—is not merely a source of fecundity and procreation as in the whole natural order. It also comprises right "from the beginning" the "nuptial" attribute, that is, the capacity to express love: that love precisely in which the man-person becomes a gift.

Sin Is Always a Defeat

Sin is always a squandering of our humanity, the squandering of our most precious values. This is the true reality, even though it may seem that sin allows us to achieve successes.

The turning away from the Father always carries with it a great destruction for whoever does so, for whoever transgresses his will and dissipates his heritage: the dignity of the human person and the heritage of grace.

The Church Preaches a Global Vision of Man

Following the example of Christ, who was sensitive to the elevation of humanity in all its aspects, the Church works for man's total well-being.

The laity have a particular part to carry out in the area of development, and they are given a special charisma in order to bring Christ's presence as servant into the sector of temporal affairs.

The human being who asks to be raised up from poverty and need is the same person who must attain redemption and eternal life. In the same way, he must contribute to development, offering the world a global vision of man and incessantly proclaiming the preeminence of spiritual values.

† † †

April

Live Christ, Proclaim Him in the First Person

Faith in the risen Christ is not the result of a technical understanding or the fruit of a scientific apparatus (1 Cor 1:26). What is asked of us is to announce the death of Jesus and proclaim his resurrection. Jesus lives. "God has raised him up, breaking the bonds of death" (Heb 2:24).

What in the beginning was but a tremulous whisper among the first witnesses quickly became transformed into a joyous experience of real life with him "with whom we have eaten and drunk . . . after he rose from the dead" (Heb 10:41f). Indeed, Christ really lives in the Church; he is in us all, bearers of hope and immortality.

If you have encountered Christ, live Christ, live with Christ! Announce him in the first person, as authentic witnesses: "For me to live is Christ" (Phil 1:21). Precisely in this is also true liberation: to proclaim Jesus free from ties, present in men who are transformed and made new creatures.

Why does our witness at times become futile? Because we present Jesus without all the attractive force of his person; without revealing the riches of the sublime ideal that following him entails; because we do not always succeed in manifesting a conviction translated in terms of life, with regard to the stupendous value of giving ourselves to the ecclesial cause we serve.

It Is Impossible to Love Christ without the Church That Christ Loves

The Church is born from the response of faith that we give to Christ. Indeed, it is by means of the sincere acceptance of the good news that we bring together believers in the name of Jesus to seek the kingdom, build it, and live it (En, no. 13). The Church is constituted by "those who look with faith to Jesus, the author of salvation and principle of unity and peace" (LG, no. 9).

On the other hand, however, we are born from the Church: she communicates to us the riches of life and grace of which she is the depositary; she generates us through baptism, nourishes us with the sacraments and the Word of God, prepares us for the mission, and guides us in fulfilling the design of God—the reason for our existence as Christians. We are her children. We call her our mother with legitimate pride, repeating a title that comes from primitive times and across the centuries.

"No one can have God for his Father unless he has the Church for his mother" (St. Cyprian). "It is impossible to love Christ without the Church that Christ loves" (EN, no. 8). "To the extent that we love the Church of Christ, we possess the Holy Spirit" (St. Augustine).

We Know We Can Count on Christ

Christ is with us. This certitude pours an immense peace and a profound joy into our hearts. We know we can count on him here and, above all, now and always. He is the friend who understands us and sustains us in dark moments, because he is "the man of sorrows who understands suffering" (Is 53:3). He is the companion along the road who restores warmth to our hearts, enlightening them about the treasures of wisdom contained in the Scriptures (cf. Lk 24:32). He is the living bread come down from heaven who can enkindle in mortal flesh the spark of life that never dies (cf. Jn 6:51).

APRIL 4

Do Not Extinguish the Joy That Is Born of Faith in Christ

Christian joy is a reality that is not easy to describe, because it is spiritual and itself forms part of the mystery. Whoever truly believes that Jesus is the incarnate Word, the Redeemer of man, cannot fail to feel within his innermost depths a sense of immense joy, which is consolation, peace, abandonment, resignation, and gladness. The Psalmist said: "Taste and see how good the Lord is!" (Ps 33:9). And the French philosopher-scientist Blaise Pascal, on the famous night of his conversion, wrote in his testament: "Joy! joy! cries of joy!"

Do not extinguish this joy that is born of faith in Christ, crucified and risen. Bear witness to your joy. Teach others to exult in this joy:

—it is the joy of the inner light on the meaning of life and history;

—it is the joy of God's presence in the soul, through "grace";

—it is the joy of God's forgiveness, through his priests, when we have unfortunately offended his infinite love and penitently return into his fatherly arms;

—it is the joy of the expectation of eternal happiness,

for which life is understood as an "exodus," a pilgrimage, although we are committed to the events of the world.

The Eucharist Makes Us Christians

The Church is realized when in fraternal union and communion we celebrate the sacrifice of the cross of Christ, when we announce "the death of the Lord until he comes," and when, profoundly permeated by the mystery of our salvation, we approach the table of the Lord in community: to draw nourishment in a sacramental way from the fruits of the propitiating holy sacrifice.

The Thorny Stem of Suffering Gives Rise to the Fragrant Rose of Joy

The banquet of Cana speaks to us of another banquet: the banquet of life at which all of us desire to be seated so as to taste a little joy. The human heart is made for joy and we must not be surprised if everyone pursues this goal.

Unfortunately, however, reality subjects so many persons to the frequently tormenting experience of sorrow: sicknesses, struggles, tragedies, hereditary weaknesses, loneliness, physical tortures, and more anguish—a fantail of concrete "human happenings" every one of which has a name, a face, and a history.

May our Lady be by their side and see that the generous wine of love may never diminish in their hearts. Love can in fact bring about the prodigy of making the fragrant rose of joy bloom on the thorny stem of suffering.

God Comes Near

The Eucharist brings us near to God in a stupendous fashion. And it is the sacrament of his proximity in encounters with man.

God in the Eucharist is precisely that God who has willed to enter into man's history. He has willed to accept humanity itself. He has willed to become man.

The sacrament of the Body and Blood continually reminds us of his divine humanity.

The Times Call for a Radical Examination of Our Relationship with Christ

We must not think even for a moment that each of us will not be interrogated, in our life, about Christ. We must not think that our times do not require, in the confrontations with each of us, an examination of awareness regarding Christ and our belonging to Christ and to his Church!

Our times do call for it—and how profoundly!

They call for it with various methods, on the basis of a diverse list of questions. At times these seem very disparate. And yet we are interrogated. And yet the examination takes place. And it is a very profound examination. Very radical.

Christ Is on the Side of Those Who Expect Love and Those Who Give Them Love

Christ is on the side of man; and he is such on both sides—on the side of those who expect solicitude, service, and charity as well as on the side of those who give service, bring solicitude, and show love.

Often Interiorization Is Sacrificed for Efficiency

A pause for true adoration has greater value and spiritual fruit than the most intense activity, even apostolic activity itself. This is the most urgent contestation that religion must make to a society in which efficiency has become an idol, on whose altar human dignity itself is frequently offered.

A Faith That Is Deep, Clear, and Certain

In order to be able truly to enlist our time and our capabilities for the salvation and sanctification of souls—the primary and principal mission of the Church—we must above all possess certitude and clarity about the truths that must be believed and practiced. If we are unsure, uncertain, confused, or contradictory, we cannot build.

Especially nowadays, we have need of an enlightened and convinced faith in order to be enlightening and convincing. The phenomenon of mass "culturalization" demands a deep, clear, and secure faith.

We Must Detach Ourselves from Our Sensuality to Enhance Our Personality

Man is a being composed of body and soul. Some contemporary writers present this structural composition of man under the form of strata and speak of external strata on the surface of our personality, opposing them to our inner strata.

Our life seems to be divided into such strata and unfolds through them. While the surface strata are linked with our sensuality, the inner strata are expressions of man's spirituality, that is, of conscious will, reflection, conscience, and the capacity to live superior values.

Man develops regularly when the inner strata of his personality finds a sufficient expression, when the circle of his interests and his aspirations is not limited only to the external and surface strata connected with human sensuality.

To facilitate such a development, we must at times knowingly separate ourselves from whatever serves to satisfy sensuality, that is, from those surface external strata.

Beauty That Does Not Vanish

We must remember that man must above all be beautiful internally. Without this beauty, all the efforts directed to the body alone will not forge—either out of him or out of her—a truly beautiful person.

Man's Encounter with God

Man knows God by encountering him and conversely he encounters God in the act of knowing.

We encounter God when we open ourselves to him with the inward gift of the human "I" to accept and reciprocate his gift.

We Play the Card of Our Life Pointing Toward Heaven

Our life is a journey toward heaven, where we will be loved and love forever and in a complete and perfect fashion. We are born solely to go to heaven.

The thought of heaven should strengthen us against temptations and make us committed to religious and moral formation, vigilant about the circle in which we live, and trusting that if we are faithful to Christ we will overcome every difficulty.

We must think of heaven! We play the card of our life pointing toward heaven!

This certitude and this expectation do not distract us from our earthly tasks; in fact, they purify these tasks and intensify them, as the life of every saint demonstrates.

The Communion of Persons Is Constructed from Within

The "affirmation of the person" is nothing more than the acceptance of the gift which—by means of reciprocity—creates the communion of persons; this is constructed from within, comprising also the whole "interiority" of man, that is, all that constitutes the pure and simple nudity of the body in its masculinity and femininity.

Whoever Squanders Condemns His Neighbor to Death

Does our heart cling to material riches? To power over others? To egotistical subtleties of domination? Then we have need of Christ the liberator who, if we want him to, can free us from these bonds of sin that hinder us.

We must get ready to allow ourselves to be enriched by the grace of the resurrection, freeing us from every false treasure: those material goods that are not necessary to us often constitute, for millions of human beings, the essential conditions for survival.

But hundreds of millions of men, besides the minimum necessary for their subsistence, look to us for aid in giving them the indispensable means for their integral human growth as well as the economic and cultural development of their countries.

Man Asks, but Does God Respond?

According to some, the silence of God characterizes our time and creates a particularly difficult climate.

But we must ask ourselves if this is really the case.

God has said everything when he has spoken through his Son, his eternal Word.

It is solely a question as to whether the power of the Word that is heard equals the fullness of the Word that is pronounced over the course of all the centuries.

The Priesthood of the Christian

Leading a life based on the sacraments, animated by the common priesthood, signifies first of all on the Christian's part a desire that God will act in him and enable him to reach "the full maturity of Christ."

God, on his part, does not touch the Christian only through events and through his inward grace but also acts in him with greater certainty and power, through the sacraments. These give his life a sacramental cast.

Among all of the sacraments, it is the Eucharist that brings to completion his initiation as a Christian and that confers on the exercise of the common priesthood this sacramental and ecclesial form that connects it with that of the ministerial priesthood. In such a way, eucharistic worship is the center of the whole sacramental life.

The Substance of the Divine Mystery

With the cross of Christ, death became the beginning of life, the superabundant source of the new life. This is the substance of the divine mystery, which animates the Church and humanity.

The Whole Gospel Is a Dialogue with Man

The whole Gospel is a dialogue with man, with the various generations, with nations, with the different traditions . . . but it is always and uninterruptedly a dialogue with man, with every man—one, unique, and absolutely singular.

At the same time, we encounter many dialogues in the Gospel. Among these I find particularly eloquent the dialogue of Christ with the rich young man.

Why did Christ dialogue with this young man? The answer is found in the evangelical text. And I am asked why—wherever I go—I want to meet the youth. I answer: because the young man is the man who in a special and decisive way is being "formed."

This does not mean that man is not formed all throughout his life; education is said to begin even before birth and to last until one's last day. However, from the viewpoint of formation, youth is a particularly rich and decisive time. And if we reflect on the dialogue of Christ with the rich young man, we will find the confirmation of what I have said to you. The questions of youth are essential, and so are the replies.

Every Threat to Human Rights Poses a Danger to Peace

Man lives simultaneously in the world of material values and in the world of spiritual values.

For the concrete person who lives and hopes, the needs, freedoms, and relations with others never correspond only with one or the other of these spheres of values but belong to both spheres.

It is legitimate to consider material goods and spiritual goods separately in order to better understand that in the concrete person they are inseparable.

Every threat to human rights, whether in the ambit of material goods or in the area of spiritual goods is equally perilous for peace, because it always concerns man in his totality.

Love Has Need of Freedom

Freedom and truth determine the spiritual imprint that marks the diverse manifestations of life and human activity.

Above all, love has need of freedom: the commitment of freedom in a certain sense constitutes its essence.

That "love" which does not have its proper source in freedom, that "love" which is not a free commitment since it is determined or the effect of compulsion, cannot be recognized as love; it contains none of love's essence.

The Laity Must Battle Against All Injustice

Particular attention must be paid to the formation of a social conscience on all levels and in all sectors.

When injustices mount and unfortunately the distance between rich and poor widens, social teaching—in a form that is creative and open to the vast areas of the Church's presence—must be the precious instrument for formation and action. This is particularly true for the laity: "The secular duties and dynamism properly pertain to the laity, although not exclusively" (GS, no. 43).

It is necessary to avoid delusions and to study seriously when certain forms of assistance have reason to exist.

The laity are indeed called, in virtue of their vocation in the Church, to make their contribution to political and economic areas, and to be effectively present in defending and promoting human rights.

Overcome Evil with Good

When innocent men die, when society lives in a state of threat, it reveals its backward side: not the struggle for man's good but the struggle against man. Is not this struggle—under various aspects—"a painful sign of the times?"

Therefore, that "sign" of "contradiction" is indispensable which was born of the prayer of Christ himself and dictated by love for man: "Do not be overcome by evil, but overcome evil with good" (Rom 12:21).

In an age when the various programs of the struggle for man take on threatening forms of the struggle against man, there is need for an effort directed to bringing men together, to their union on the basis of what is essentially and profoundly human.

Christ Teaches Us to Become the Man for Others

If you ask me what the youth must do in the Church, I will reply: Learn to know Christ. Grasp Christ. In him are found truly unfathomable riches of wisdom and knowledge. In him man weighed down by limits, vices, weakness, and sin becomes truly "a new man."

He becomes "the man for others"; he also becomes the glory of God, since the glory of God—as the bishop and martyr St. Irenaeus of Lyons declared in the second century—is "living man." The experience of two millennia teaches us that in this basic work, the mission of the whole people of God, there is no essential difference between man and woman.

The Generous Capacity for Commitment on the Part of Young People Has Not Worn Out

Youth is disposed to respond. Its generous capacity to be committed to noble ideals even at the cost of sacrifice is not worn out.

Let us know how to transmit to that youth, without dilution or false modesty, the great values of the Gospel and the example of Christ.

These are causes that the young person perceives as worthy of being lived and as ways of responding to God and his fellow man.

Dialogue with One's Brothers Does Not Efface One's Identity

The quest for ecclesial unity leads to the heart of ecumenism. Prayer, trust, and fidelity must be the climate of authentic ecumenism.

The dialogue between brothers of different confessions does not efface but presupposes our own identity.

The Church Helps Us to See and Respect Every Man as a Brother

The Church inscribes herself in the reality of peoples: in their culture, in their history, and in the rhythm of their development. She lives in profound solidarity with the sorrows of her children, sharing their difficulties and taking up their legitimate aspirations.

Serving the cause of justice, the Church does not intend to provoke or heighten divisions, to worsen conflicts or make them greater.

With the power of the Gospel, the Church helps us to see and respect every man as a brother, invites persons, groups, and peoples to dialogue so that justice may be safeguarded and unity maintained.

Do Not Shut Yourselves Up Within Yourselves: Think of the Most Poor

The Church—which wants to be the Church of the poor—says to those who live in abundance, or at least in a relative well-being and have what is necessary (even if at times they lack what is superfluous!): Enjoy the fruits of your work and a legitimate industriousness. But in the name of the words of Christ, in the name of human fraternity and social solidarity, do not shut yourselves up within yourselves.

Think of the most poor! Think of those who lack what is sufficient, who live in chronic misery, who suffer hunger! And share with them! Share with them in a programmed and systematic way. Do not let material abundance separate you from the beatitudes of the Sermon on the Mount.

† † †

May

Work—Service for Mankind

Christian doctrine on man, nourished by the Gospel, the Bible, and centuries of experience, gives value to human work in a singular fashion. The dignity of work. The nobility of work.

Work is a service in which man himself grows to the extent that he gives himself for others. It is a discipline in which personality becomes strengthened.

Justice demands that the conditions of work be the most suitable possible, that social planning be perfected so as to permit all—on the basis of a growing solidarity—to face social risks, distresses, and burdens.

Do Everything Possible to Make Women Merit Love and Respect

Motherhood is woman's vocation. It is an eternal vocation. "The mother who knows everything and with her heart embraces each of us": these are the words of a song sung by the youth in Poland.

The song goes on to mention that today the world "hungers and thirsts" for that motherhood that "physically" and "spiritually" is the vocation of women, as it is of Mary.

We must do everything possible so that the dignity of this splendid vocation will not be broken within the interior life of the new generations; so that the authority of the woman-mother will not be diminished in family, social, and public life as well as in our entire civilization; in all our contemporary legislation, in the organization of work, in publications, in the culture of everyday life, in education, and in study. In every sphere of life. This is a fundamental criterion.

We must do everything possible to ensure that women merit love and respect. We must do everything possible to make children, the family, and society see in her that dignity which Christ has seen!

The Ineradicable Dignity of Those Not Yet Born

How can we fail to reaffirm solemnly that the life of the human being is sacred from his emergence under his mother's heart at the moment of conception? How can we forget that the number of lives snuffed out in the maternal womb has reached frightful proportions?

It is a silent slaughter than cannot leave indifferent not only we men of the Church, we Christians of the whole world, but even those responsible for the public realm, and those concerned with the future of nations.

In the name of Jesus "living in Mary" (Ven. Olier), borne by her in her womb into the indifferent and hostile world—at Bethlehem he was refused acceptance and in the palace his death was plotted—in the name of that child, God and man, I adjure those who are aware of the ineradicable dignity of the persons not yet born to take a position worthy of man, that this tragic period which threatens to envelop the human conscience in darkness may finally be overcome.

The Child, a New Revelation of Life

The child is always a new revelation of life, which is given man by the Creator. It is a new confirmation of the image and likeness of God imprinted on men from the very beginning.

The child is also a powerful and continual verification of our faithfulness to ourselves and of our faithfulness to humanity. It is a verification of respect for the mystery of life, upon which from the very moment of conception the Creator inscribes the imprint of his image and likeness.

The dignity of the child demands a very lively sensitivity of conscience on the part of the parents and society. For the child is the focal point that fashions or disrupts the morality of families, and in consequence the morality of entire nations and of societies.

The dignity of the child demands the greatest responsibility on the part of parents and also the greatest social responsibility in every sector.

The Family, Community of Love

In a world where the enduring function of many institutions seems to be lessening and the quality, especially of urban life, is deteriorating in a striking fashion, the family can and must become a place of true peace and harmonious growth. It must do so not to isolate itself in the form of haughty self-sufficiency but to offer the world a luminous testimony of the great possibility for the recuperation and integral advancement of man if it has as point of departure and reference the healthy vitality of the primary cell of the civic and ecclesial fabric.

Therefore, it is necessary that the Christian family be transformed ever more into a community of love, such as to allow the inevitable trials that arise from daily concerns to be overcome through fidelity and harmony; a community of life in order to give origin to and joyously cultivate new and precious human existences in the image of God; and a community of grace that will continually make the Lord Jesus Christ the proper center of gravitation and the precise power point so as to fructify the obligations of each one and acquire new vigor on each day's journey.

MAY 6

Love Designates the Place of Man in the Reign of God

Man's greatest vocation is the call to love. Love even gives definitive meaning to human life.

It is the essential condition for the dignity of man, the proof of his nobility of soul. St. Paul would say that it is "the bond of perfection" (Col 3:14).

It is the greatest thing in the life of man, because—true love—it bears within itself the dimension of eternity. It is immortal: "Love will never end," we read in the First Letter to the Corinthians (13:8).

Man dies as far as the body is concerned, because that is the destiny of everyone on earth; however, this death does not harm the love that has matured during his life.

MAY 7

Without Love We Remain Incomprehensible Even to Ourselves

We cannot live without love.

If we do not encounter love, if we do not experience it

and make it our own, and if we do not share intimately in love, our life has no meaning.

Without love we remain incomprehensible even to ourselves.

If Justice Vacillates Even Love Is in Danger

There can be no love without justice. Love "oversees" justice but, at the same time, finds its verification in justice. If justice vacillates even love is in danger.

MAY 9

The Fragile Construction of the "Fiction" of Love

Egotism of the senses or feelings can be hidden only for a short time, concealed in the folds of a "fiction" called, with apparent good faith, "love."

But the fragility of this construction is destined to fatally manifest itself one day.

And it is one of the greatest sufferings to see love reveal itself as the opposite of what one believed it to be.

MAY 10

The Eucharist Arises Out of Love and Serves Love

Eucharistic worship is the expression of love, and it is the authentic and most profound characteristic of the Christian vocation. This worship arises out of love and serves love—to which all of us are called in Jesus Christ.

Man Has Immense Reserves of Goodness

If humanity wishes to control an evolution that slips out of our hands; if it wishes to withdraw itself from the materialistic temptation that gains ground in a desperate flight forward; if it wishes to assure the authentic development of men and peoples—it must radically revise its conceptions of progress, which under various names have caused spiritual values to atrophy.

The Church offers her help. She does not shrink from denunciation of outrages to human dignity. However, she conserves her main energies to help men and human groups, employers and workers. She wants them to be conscious of the immense reserves of goodness that they have within themselves and that they have already caused to bear fruit in their history.

The Receptacle of Every Action of God Is Man

Possibly the most striking weakness of present civilization consists in its inadequate vision of man. Ours is undoubtedly the age in which much has been written and spoken about man, the age of humanisms and anthropocentrism. Yet, paradoxically, it is also the age of man's deepest anxieties on previously unsuspected levels, the age of human values spurned as never before.

How can we explain this paradox? We can say that it is a question of the inexorable paradox of atheistic humanism. It is the drama of man cut off from an essential dimension of his being—his quest for the infinite—and so placed before the worst reduction of himself. The pastoral Constitution *Gaudium et Spes* teaches the basis of the problem when it states: "Solely in the mystery of the Incarnate Word does the mystery of man take on its true light" (GS, no. 22).

The Church, thanks to the Gospel, possesses the truth about man. This is found in anthropology, which the Church never ceases to study and to communicate. The primordial affirmation of such anthropology is that of man as the image of God, irreducible to a simple particle of nature or to an anonymous element of the human city (GS, nos. 12, 3 and 14, 2). In this sense, St. Irenaeus writes: "Man's glory is God, but the receptacle of every action of God, of his wisdom and of his power, is man."

MAY 13

Humility Is Rejection of Superficiality

Humility is not identified with humiliation or with resignation. It does not go hand in hand with pusillanimity.

To the contrary. Humility is creative submission to the power of truth and love.

Humility is rejection of affectation and superficiality; it is the expression of the depth of the human spirit; it is a condition of its greatness.

MAY 14

The Rosary—Opening One's Soul to the Holy Spirit

The rosary, slowly recited and meditated upon in the family, in the community, or individually, will enable you to enter little by little into the sentiments of Christ and his mother, recalling all the events that are the key to our salvation.

On the wave of the Ave Maria, you will contemplate the mystery of the incarnation of Christ, the redemption of

Christ, and also the goal to which we tend, in the light and rest of God.

With Mary, you will open your soul to the Holy Spirit, so that he may inspire all the great tasks that await you. With him, mothers will fulfill their role as life-bearers, custodians, and educators of the hearth. May Mary be your guide and your sustenance.

The Wonders of the "Fiat" of Mary Immaculate

O Mary conceived without sin, pray for us who have recourse to you.

You have been so closely associated with the whole work of our redemption, associated with the cross of our Savior. Your heart was pierced by it, beside his heart. And now, in the glory of your Son, you do not cease to intercede for us, poor sinners.

You watch over the Church and are the mother of the Church. You watch over each of your children. You obtain for us from God all of those graces symbolized by the rays of light emanating from your open hands.

The sole condition on our part is that we come to you with confidence, with boldness, and with the simplicity of a child.

God Begins to Make Us Grow from Within

[Lord,] you further your plan. . . .

You could be termed implacable, in the sense that you are resolute: your plans are irreversible. Stranger than everything is the fact that this becomes evident only at the end: that is, that you hardly every struggle with me. You enter by force only into what I call my solitude and shatter the obstinacy that is connected with it in me. But is it really true that you enter by force? Or is it perhaps that you enter by a door that is ever open?

You have not created me closed; you have not shut me up tight. The desire for solitude is not quite complete but always springs up from some opening in my being that is much wider than I could ever imagine. You enter precisely through it and slowly begin to make me grow from within.

The Value of Man Is Measured by the Death of Christ

The man who wants to understand himself in depth— not only according to immediate, partial, often superficial, and even visible criteria and measures of his own being— must, with his anxiety and uncertainty as well as his own weakness and sinfulness, draw close to Christ.

He must, so to speak, enter into him with all of himself; he must "appropriate" and assimilate the whole reality of the incarnation and the redemption in order to rediscover himself.

If this profound process takes place in him, he will bear fruits not only of adoration of God but also of profound wonder toward himself.

What great value must a man have in the eyes of the Creator if "he has merited to have so noble and great a Redeemer," if "God has given his Son" so that he, man, "may not perish but may possess life eternal!"

We Must Bow Our Head Before Our Suffering Brother or Sister

The suffering of a neighbor, the suffering of another man, like me in everything, always creates in those who do not suffer a certain uneasiness, almost a sense of embarrassment. They instinctively pose the question: Why that person and not me?

It is not legitimate to shrink from this question, for it is the basic expression of human solidarity.

We must pause before suffering, before a person who is suffering, in order to discover that essential bond between my human "I" and his.

We must pause before the person who is suffering, to bear witness to him—and, insofar as possible together with him, to all the dignity of suffering—I might say, the whole majesty of suffering.

We must bow our head before brothers or sisters who are weak and defenseless, deprived even of what has been given to us and which we enjoy every day.

These are only a few aspects of that great trial that costs man so dearly but at the same time purifies him, as it purifies the person who seeks to be united with the other, with the suffering human "I."

Christ has said: "I was sick and you visited me" (Mt 25:36).

"Confess" Christ "The Son of the Living God"

We must confess Christ before history and the world with deep, strong, and lively conviction in the manner of

Peter: "You are the Messiah, the Son of the living God" (Mt 16:18).

This is the good news in a certain unique sense: the Church lives by means of it and through it, just as she draws from it all that she has to offer to men, without any distinction of nationality, culture, race, time, epoch, or condition.

This is the unique Gospel, and "even if we ourselves or an angel from heaven should preach to you another Gospel, let him be anathema," as the Apostle has clearly stated.

MAY 20

Man "Sees" Himself in Christ

The Church, as the body of Christ and his faithful bride, the Church as the people of God, can never depart from the past of tradition, but neither can she be content simply to look to the past. The "Backward-looking Church" must also look to the future ("Forward-looking Church").

The Church must reveal to this future—and to the men who are already living as well as those who are to come—Jesus Christ, full and unadulterated mystery of salvation.

This mystery is an eternal mystery in God, who wants all men to be saved and to come to the knowledge of the truth. It is the mystery that has become in time a divine-human reality that bears the name of Jesus Christ.

It is a reality that does not come to rest outside of man; the reason for its existence is to be and to operate in man; to build the fount and the ferment of the new life in every man.

To evangelize means to go in this direction, so that the fount and the ferment of the new life may shine forth in men and in ever new generations.

To evangelize does not mean merely to speak "about Christ." To proclaim Christ signifies to enable man—the one addressed by this announcement—"to believe," that is, to see himself in Christ; to rediscover in Christ the adequate dimension of his own life. In short, it means to rediscover himself in Christ.

Through What Is Obscure in Us to Reveal What Is Luminous

How many years will a man at times dedicate to clarifying some fact for himself, to discovering the answer to a specific question!

And how much effort must each one of us put forth so that we can—through all that is "obscure" and dark in us, through the whole "worst part of our self," through the man overcome by the concupiscence of the flesh, the eyes, and the pride of life (1 Jn 2:16)—reveal what is luminous: the man of simplicity, humility, love, and disinterested sacrifice; the new horizons of mind, heart, will, and character.

Man, Life, and Death

Although man does not choose his own death, nevertheless by choosing a certain form of life he—in this perspective and in a certain sense—chooses even his own death.

We Are Poor, but We Are Rich

It is necessary to recall and to repeat to the men of our time: the Bridegroom is with you! You are loved even to the extent of a complete and definitive giving.

This is the heritage Christ has left us: love for every human being. A patrimony that is seemingly poor but is in reality the most powerful. For what does man desire if not to be loved? What gives fundamental meaning to our existence if not this?

We are poor, but we are rich. The Bridegroom is with us!

Behind Man Is God

Man, independently of his great weakness, his great littleness, and all his deficiencies, is great.

Behind him there is God.

God has become man.

Only the Poor in Spirit Are Ready for the Wonderful Works of God

The poor in spirit are those who are open to God and to "the wonderful works of God" (Acts 2:11). They are poor because they are always ready to welcome that gift from on high which comes from God himself.

Poor in spirit are those who live with the awareness of

having received everything from God's hands as a free gift and who prize every good received. Continually grateful, they repeat without ceasing, "All is grace." "Let us give thanks to the Lord our God."

Jesus once described them as "pure of heart" and "meek"; it is they who "hunger and thirst for justice," they who are constantly "sorrowful," they who are "peacemakers," and "persecuted for the sake of justice." It is they, finally, who are "the merciful" (cf. Mt 5:3–10).

Hearts That Are Open to God Are Open to Men

The poor in spirit are also those most open to men. They are ready to help and to lend themselves, ready to give what they have, ready to welcome an abandoned widow or orphan into their home.

They always find one more place amid the straitened circumstances in which they exist. And in this spirit they know how to find a piece of bread and a little food on their poor table.

Woe to the "Rich Man" Closed to God and to Men

Are the words of Christ concerning the poor in spirit likely to make us forget injustices? Do they allow us to leave unresolved the various problems that arise at the core of the so-called social problem?

These words do not seek to do away with social problems: on the contrary, they highlight these problems, focusing them on the most essential point which is man, which is the heart of man, which is every man without exception.

Man before God and at the same time man before other men.

Does not poor in spirit signify precisely "the man open to others," that is, to God and neighbor?

Is it not true that this expression says to those who are not "poor in spirit" that they are outside the reign of God and that they are not and will not be participants in this reign?

Thinking of these men, who are "rich," closed to God and men, will not Christ cry out on another occasion: "Woe to you"?

Man Is Measured Not by What He Has but by What He Is

The Church of the poor says to those who live in abundance, who live in luxury: Look around you a little! Doesn't your heart grieve? Don't you feel remorse of conscience because of your riches and your abundance?

Nonetheless, if you want only "to have" ever more, if your idols are lucre and pleasure, remember that the value of man is measured not by what he "has" but by what he "is."

The measure of riches, money, and luxury does not equal the measure of man's true dignity.

Popular Religiosity Expresses the Very Soul of Peoples

Among the elements for a pastoral that bears the stamp of love for the poor are the following: the concern for a solid and accessible preaching; for a catechesis that embraces the whole Christian message; for a liturgy that respects the sense of the sacred and avoids the risks of political instrumentalization; for a familial pastoral that defends the poor from unjust campaigns harmful to their dignity; for education, so that it may reach the least favorable sectors, and for popular religiosity in which is expressed the very soul of peoples.

There Is No Cross Without Christ and No Christ Without a Cross

Two attitudes are possible toward the cross, and both are dangerous. The first consists in seeking in the cross whatever is oppressive and painful, to the point of taking pleasure in sorrow and suffering, as if they possessed a value in themselves.

The second attitude is that of refusing the cross and succumbing to the mystique of hedonism and glory, pleasure and power.

A great spiritual writer, Fulton Sheen, used to speak in this respect of those who cling to a cross without Christ in contrast to those who seem to want a Christ without the cross.

The Christian knows that man's Redeemer is a Christ on the cross, and therefore only with Christ is the cross redemptive!

Without a Change of Heart and Conscience There Will Be No Just Social Order

Those who are economically well off must acquire the spirit of poverty—they must open their heart to the poor. If they fail to do so, unjust situations will not change.

The political structure or the social system may change. But without a change of heart and conscience, a just and stable social order will never be attained.

† † †

June

It Is Truth That Makes Us Free

Liberation signifies man's inner transformation, which is the consequence of the knowledge of truth. Hence, transformation is a spiritual process in which man grows "in justice and true holiness" (Eph 4:24).

Man thus mature internally becomes the representative and spokesman of this "justice and true holiness" in the various spheres of social life.

Truth is not only important for the growth of human awareness, thus deepening man's internal life. Truth also has a prophetic significance and power. It constructs the content of bearing witness and demands a witness.

We find this prophetic power of truth in the teachings of Christ. As a prophet, as the witness to truth, Christ repeatedly opposes himself to non-truth; he does so with great power and decisiveness and often does not hesitate to censure what is false.

Let us reread the Gospel accurately. We will find therein not a few expressions of severity, for example, "whitened sepulchers," "blind guides," and "hypocrites," which Christ voices in the full awareness of the consequences that await him.

Truth Is Not an Object of "Prizes and Competition"

Service to truth as a share in the prophetic service of Christ is a task of the Church, who seeks to fulfill it in the various historical contexts. It is necessary to call by their true name all injustice, all exploitation of man by the state, by institutions, by mechanisms of economic systems, or by regimes operating at times without sensitivity. It is necessary to call by name all social injustice, discrimination, and violence inflicted on man against the body, against the spirit, against his conscience, and against his convictions.

Christ teaches us a particular sensitivity toward man, toward the dignity of the human person, toward human life, toward the spirit and the human body.

It is not permitted to man to hide this truth before him. It is not permitted to "falsify it." It is not permitted to make of this truth an object of "prizes and competition."

It is necessary to speak about it in a clear and simple fashion. And not to "censure men but to serve the cause of man." Liberation, even in the social sense, starts with the recognition of truth.

The "Logic of Love" in Creation

A single logic rules all creation from the very beginning. It is a "logic of love," which may perhaps be equated with the logic of which Pascal spoke: "The heart has its own reasons." Exactly, the heart! Throughout the whole narrative of Genesis we hear the beating of a heart!

The Power to Be Man

The person who is born in all the weakness of man is born to help me to be a man, to give me the power to be a man.

To be fully a man signifies being a child of God, because the Son of God has become man.

Permit Christ to Speak to Man

Nowadays, very often man does not know what he bears within himself, in the depths of his spirit and his heart. Very often he is uncertain about the meaning of his life on this earth. He is pervaded by doubt that becomes desperation. Therefore, I beg you, I implore you, with humility and trust, permit Christ to speak to man. He alone has the words of life—yes, of eternal life.

The Priest, Man of Hope

In pastoral, the inevitable difficulties must not shake our trust. "We know that Christ has risen from the dead." The presence of the risen Christ is the secure foundation of a hope "that does not disappoint" (Rom 5:5).

That is why the priest must be, always and everywhere, a man of hope. It is true that the world is pierced by profound tensions that very often generate difficulties whose immediate solution is above our possibilities. In such circumstances and at every moment, it is necessary for the priest to know how to offer his brothers, by word and example, convincing reasons for hope. And he can do so because his certitudes are not founded on human opinions but on the solid rock of God's Word.

JUNE 7

The Priest, Man for God and for Others

As the Mediator, the Lord Jesus was, in all the dimensions of his being, the man for God and for others. The same is true of the priest; and this is why he is asked to consecrate his whole life to God and to the Church, in the depths of his being, his faculties, and his sentiments.

The priest, who by choosing celibacy renounces human love so as to offer himself completely to the love of God, gains the freedom to give himself to others by a gift that does not exclude any person but includes all in the flow of charity that comes from God (cf. Rom 5:5) and leads to God. Celibacy, by binding the priest to God, frees him to give himself to all the works demanded by the care of souls.

JUNE 8

In Everyone There Is Something Which Indicates Christ— Always

Deepen your knowledge of Christ by heeding the words of the Lord's ministers and reading some pages of the Gospel. Seek to discover where he is and you will be able to get from everyone some particular characteristic that will indicate him to you, that will tell you where he dwells. Seek him in the meek, the penitent, the generous, the humble and hidden; seek him in your brothers, near and far, for in each you will find something that will indicate Jesus to you.

Seek him above all in your soul and your conscience, for they will be able to indicate in an unmistakable manner the sound of his footsteps, the imprint of his passage, the trace of his power and love. However, seek him with humility: that is, your soul must be disposed to see, outside itself, what God has sown of his goodness in creatures.

To seek him every day means to possess him a little more every day, to be admitted a little at a time into intimacy with him. Thus you can better grasp the sound of his voice, the meaning of his language, the reason for his coming on earth and his immolation on the cross.

JUNE 9

Man Seeks God because He Bears Within Himself the Image of God

Man desires God and seeks him until he finds him. This is a basic truth about man, a kind of measure of humanity, a verification of man's greatness.

It is obvious that there are men who say: I do not find, I do not know how to reach, I do not know how to find. There are also those to whom grace has been given and who have found, and who at times squander it without thinking and easily lose it.

All of this is part of the truth of the human soul, of the historical truth and the daily truth about man. All of this speaks in a particular way about his greatness. It says that he has been created in the image and likeness of God.

Man seeks God because he bears within himself God's image and likeness and finds the fulfillment of his definitive goal only in him according to whose image and likeness he is made.

Christ Brings Man Freedom Founded on Truth

Even today, after two thousand years, Christ comes to us as the one who brings man freedom founded on truth, as the one who frees man from what sets limits to, minimizes, and as it were shatters this freedom at its very roots, in man's soul, in his heart, in his conscience.

What a stupendous confirmation of this those persons have given and do not cease to give who, thanks to Christ, and in Christ, have attained true freedom and manifested it even in conditions of external constraint!

Man Must Be a "Confessor"

Man cannot be tepid or disillusioned; he must be a confessor, because it is in his confession, [that is, his act of bearing witness] that is manifested, his total relationship with truth and with the God who is truth.

Life, Man's Great Proving Ground

Life is man's great proving ground. And it is precisely because of this that man has a meaning. He has no meaning, on the other hand, if we think that during life man must only make a profit, use, and "amass," and indeed fight tenaciously for the right to make a profit, use, and "amass."

Life has a meaning when it is looked upon and lived as a proving ground of ethical character. Christ confirms this meaning and, at the same time, defines the adequate dimension of this proving ground that is human life. Let us accurately reread, for example, the Sermon on the Mount and Chapter 25 of Matthew's gospel: the image of the judgment. This alone is enough to renew in us the fundamental Christian awareness of the meaning of life.

The idea of a proving ground is closely linked with the idea of responsibility. Both are directed to our wills, to our actions.

We must accept both of these ideas—or rather both of these realities—as elements in the building up of our own humanity.

The Hours Become Psalms

Weak is the people when it consents to defeat, when it loses sight of its mission to be vigilant until the hour arrives. The hours always reappear on the great clock of history.

This is the liturgy of events. Vigilance is the word of the Lord and also the word of the people, and we will always embrace both. The hours become a psalm of incessant conversions. Let us go to celebrate the Eucharist of the world.

The Power of Prayer Is the Power of God

Prayer is a constitutive element of human existence in the world, which is "to be toward God." At the same time, it is a kind of "being in the dimensions of God," a humble but daring insertion of self in the profundity of God's thought, his majesty, and his plans.

Prayer is in some way a "touching" of the very fount of the divine power: will and grace.

Prayer is the power of the weak, and the weakness of the strong.

Prayer is the first expression of man's inner truth, the first condition of the authentic freedom of the spirit.

Prayer is always a wonderful reduction of eternity to the dimension of a concrete moment, a reduction of the eternal Wisdom to the dimension of human knowledge, to the concrete way of understanding and feeling, a reduction of eternal love to the dimension of the concrete human heart, which at times is not capable of grasping its richness and seems to break.

To Pray Is to Build the Family and Make the Community

Prayer ennobles and elevates the Christian, placing him in an attitude of submission and gratitude to God, who has given himself completely to men, making them share in his divine life through his Son.

Can there be a greater and more intimate communication than this? By means of personal prayer, by means of prayer in families, and even more by means of liturgical prayer, man is reborn every day, in the measure that he assimilates the divine gifts and renders them alive in his conduct to the extent of becoming truly a familiar and an intimate of God.

To pray is to build a family, make a community, and become rooted salutarily in the new and definitive covenant, sealed by Christ in the sacrament of love, the Eucharist.

Good Is Spread Outwardly Beginning from "Within"

Man, human life and all that is human, is formed first from within. And according to what is in man, in his conscience and in his heart, is fashioned his whole eternal life as well as his life in common with others.

If in man there is good—a sense of justice as well as love, chastity, benevolence toward others, and a healthy desire for dignity—this good radiates outside of him and forms the face of families, circles, and institutions.

We Must Know How to Acquire Freedom

Freedom is offered to us and is conferred on us like a mission. Not only must we possess it, but we must also know how to acquire it.

We must construct our own existence by directing it toward the good in an increasing right use of our freedom.

This is the real essence, the fundamental task on which depend both the meaning and the value of our whole life.

The Ultimate Question Is Always a Question About God

Particular truths are not enough for us, even if in every field of human activity we seek the truth. Truth becomes for us a source of inspiration in work, in science.

Nevertheless, the hunger for the truth in our souls goes further. The ultimate question is always a question about

God, it is always a question about the meaning of human life, about the beginning and especially about the end of the road that we traverse on earth.

A Climate of Falsehood Is Always Against the Human

Truth is like the star to which we turn our soul's gaze.

We must live by the truth, we must seek it, we must tend toward it. We cannot make any sense of or live by falsehood.

A climate of falsehood is always a climate against the human.

Freedom Is Achieved in Giving and in Service

In our day there is at times the erroneous notion that freedom is an end in itself, that everyone is free when he uses freedom as he wishes, and that this is the goal toward which the life of individuals and societies should tend.

In reality, however, freedom is a great gift only when we know how to use it consciously for what is the true good.

Christ teaches us that the best use of freedom is charity, which is achieved in giving and in service.

The Family Has Its Beginning in the Motherhood of the Mother

The family has its beginning in the motherhood of the mother, and motherhood has its beginning in the conception of a human being, in the conception of a baby.

In conceiving a baby, the woman becomes a mother; she enters into the mystery of her own motherhood. In the dimensions of human relations, she makes a gift of this motherhood to her husband, and he attains the dignity of fatherhood as a result of her motherhood.

Such is the moral order of this fundamental, eternal, and immutable event in the history of man.

The Beginning of Man Takes Place in the Heart of His Mother

I wish to pay honor to motherhood and to the faith in man that it entails.

To pay honor to motherhood signifies an acceptance of man in all his truth and in all his dignity from the very first moment of his existence. The beginning of man takes place in the heart of his mother.

Everything Depends on the Family

The family is the first and fundamental human community.

It is the environment of life and the environment of love. The life of every society, nation, and state depends on the family—if, that is, the family is in their midst a true environment of life and love.

It is necessary to do much, and indeed to do everything possible, to give the family the conditions required for this: working conditions, housing conditions, maintenance conditions, care for conceived life, social respect for fatherhood and motherhood, joy provided by babies who come into the world, full right to education as well as help under various forms for education. . . .

This is a vast and rich program on which man's future depends.

God Constitutes a Family

It is said in a beautiful and profound way that our God in his most intimate mystery is not a hermit—rather he constitutes a family. For he has in himself fatherhood, sonship, and love, which are the essence of a family.

This love in the divine family is the Holy Spirit.

Impurity Arises in the Will

The human body in itself is not impure and neither are the reactions of sensuality and sensuality itself. Impurity arises in the will, which reduces the other person—because of his body and sex—to the rank of an object of pleasure.

Violence Destroys What It Seeks to Create

The common good of society, which will always be the new name of justice, cannot be attained by means of violence, because the latter destroys what it seeks to create—both when it seeks to preserve the privileges of some and when it attempts to impose necessary changes.

The changes demanded by a just social order must be brought about by means of a constant action—one that is often gradual and progressive but always efficacious—along the path of peaceful reforms.

The Word of the Cross, Final Cry of Love

Contemporary man is experiencing the threat of a spiritual impassibility, and even the death of the conscience. This death is something more profound than sin; it is the destruction of the sense of sin.

So many factors concur nowadays in bringing about the death of conscience in men of our time, and this corresponds to that reality that Christ has called "the sin against the Holy Spirit."

This sin begins when man no longer hears the word of the cross as the final cry of love which has the power to pierce hearts.

God Is Always First

Every man, already before beginning to seek, finds God. If he were not to find him in something signified that he uses as a starting point and a base, he would not seek.

A "Grace" to Revive Every Day

To belong to the Church, to live in the Church, and to be the Church is nowadays something very demanding.

At times, it is not very costly in the way of overt and direct persecution but it can be very costly in the way of scorn, indifference, and ostracism. In addition, there is a likely and frequent danger of fear, weariness, and insecurity.

Do not let yourselves be overcome by these temptations. Do not allow any of these sentiments to lessen the vigor and spiritual energy of your "being Church." It is a grace that we must request and be ready to receive with great inner poverty, and be prepared to revive every day, always with deeper fervor and greater intensity.

JUNE 30

God Calls Us and Knows Us

The reign of God is among you! This is the inexhaustible source of our joy: the knowledge that God calls us and knows us; the knowledge that we are free from sin, that we have been raised to the insuperable dignity of children of God, rich in faith, hope, and love, which the Holy Spirit pours out into our hearts.

† † †

July

The Choice of God Is Called Man

In his eternal love, God has chosen man from all eternity: he has chosen him in his Son. God has chosen man so that he may reach the fullness of good by sharing in God's own life, the divine life, by means of grace. He has chosen man from eternity and irreversibly.

Neither original sin nor the whole history of personal faults and social sins has been able to dissuade the eternal Father from his plan of love.

These have not been able to annul the choice of us in the eternal Son, the consubstantial Word with the Father. Because this choice was to take form in the incarnation, and because the Son of God was to become man for our salvation, the eternal Father precisely for this reason has chosen a mother for him from among men.

Every one of us becomes man by being conceived in and born from the maternal womb. The eternal Father has chosen the same path for the humanity of his eternal Son. He has chosen his mother from the people to whom for centuries he had entrusted in a particular way his mysteries and his promises. He chose her from the race of David and at the same time from all humanity. He chose her from royal stock and at the same time from the poor.

Christ Fights by Our Side for Peace

Failures will not be able to render works for peace vain, even if immediate results are fragile, even if we are persecuted because of our witness to peace. Christ the Savior unites with his destiny all those who work with love for peace.

The Challenge of Peace

Peace has become the slogan that reassures or that seeks to seduce. . . . But to take up the challenge that imposes itself on all mankind, in the face of the difficult task of peace, words are not enough, whether they be sincere or demagogic.

In particular, it is necessary that the true spirit of peace penetrate the level of political men as well as environments or centers that are more or less secretly responsible for decisive steps toward peace.

At the minimum, it is necessary that there be accord on being guided by some elementary but firm principles such as the following. The affairs of people must be settled by humanity and not by violence. Tensions, disputes, and conflicts must be regulated by reasonable negotiations and not by force. Ideological oppositions must be confronted in a climate of dialogue and free discussion. The legitimate interests of specific groups must take into account also the legitimate interests of other groups equally concerned and the higher demands of the common good. Recourse to arms cannot be considered a suitable means of resolving conflicts. Indefeasible human rights must be safeguarded in every circumstance. It is not permitted to kill in order to impose a solution.

Every man of good will can rediscover these principles of humanity in his conscience. They correspond to the will of God for men, and in order for them to become solid convictions among the powerful and the weak so as to impregnate all actions, they must again be given their whole force. A patient and lengthy education is needed at every level.

July 4

Man the Director of the Macrocosm and the Microcosm

Man must grow and develop as a man. He must grow and develop starting from the divine foundation of his humanity, that is to say, as the likeness and image of God himself. He must grow and develop as an adoptive child of God.

As the adoptive child of God, man must grow and develop by means of everything that concurs in his development and his progress in the world that he inhabits.

He must do so by means of all the works of his hands and his genius; by means of the successes of contemporary science and the application of modern technology; by means of all that he knows in regard to the macrocosm and the microcosm, thanks to an ever more perfected arrangement.

July 5

The True Christian Is Always a "Successful" Person

A true Christian—that is, a saint—is always at the same time a perfectly "successful" person. I could give you so many names, but all of them derive their greatness from a single name, which is the name of Jesus of Nazareth, Son of God from eternity who became our Lord through his death and resurrection. His life, as you are well aware, was totally spent on behalf of others until the very end.

Hence, it is to him that you must look, him that you must have in your thoughts and affections, and him that you must follow every day, because it is only about him that each of us can say with full truth in unison with St. Paul: "He has loved me and delivered himself up for me" (Gal 2:20).

It is from this that your deepest joy must come so that it will also become your strength and consequently your sustenance.

If, through misfortune, you should encounter grief, endure sufferings, experience misunderstandings, and even fall into sin, immediately let your thought of faith go to the one who always loves you. Precisely by his love that is unlimited as is that of God, he enables us to overcome every trial, fills our emptinesses, cancels every sin of ours, and impels us with enthusiasm toward a path that is newly secure and joyful.

The Christian—Interpreter and Guide

The human person attains his full self-realization only in relation to him who represents the constitutive reason for all our judgments about existence, good, truth, and beauty.

The infinite transcendence of this God, whom someone has termed the "Totally Other," has come near to us in Jesus Christ, made flesh in order to participate completely in our history. We must therefore conclude that the Christian faith enables us believers to interpret—better than any other—the most profound solicitations of the human being and to discover with serenity and tranquil security the ways and means of a full satisfaction.

JULY 7

Christ Does Not Mortify Man

Adherence to Christ does not mortify but strengthens the sense of moral duty, conferring the desire and the satisfaction to be committed through "something that is truly worthwhile," and warning the spirit against the tendencies, nowadays not rarely springing up in the youthful spirit, "to let oneself go": in the direction of an irresponsible and indolent abdication, or in the way of blind and homicidal violence.

JULY 8

Rights and Functions of State and Church

The Church is a spiritual institution, even though its expression is also social; it goes beyond temporal countries since it is a community of believers. The state is an expression of the sovereign self-determination of peoples and nations, and it constitutes a normal realization of the social order; from this comes its moral authority. An awareness of this difference of nature will eliminate all confusion and allow us to proceed with clarity.

This entails recognizing the proper character of the Church, which does not depend on a civil or political structure. And it entails recognizing the state's right to exercise its sovereignty in its own territory, and recognizing its leaders' responsibility to work for the common good of the people whom they represent.

The Place of Each Person in the Universal Church

Each of us has a unique place in the communion of the universal Church spread throughout the world. You lay people who pursue a vocation of holiness and love have a particular responsibility for the consecration of the world. Through you the Gospel must reach all levels of society.

In imitation of the Holy Family, both parents and children among you must construct a community of love and understanding in which the joys and hopes, as well as the sufferings of life, are shared and offered to God in prayer.

You who are married must be signs of God's faithful and indestructible love for his people and Christ's love for the Church. It is you who have the grand mission of giving Christ to one another, and giving him to your children. In this sense, you are the first catechists of your children.

And you young people who are preparing for the priesthood or the religious life are called to believe in Christ's power of grace over your lives. The Lord needs you to further the work of the redemption among your brothers and sisters.

Evangelization Makes Humanity New

Education in the faith posits the moral bases for a better and truly renewed social life. And Christians initiated into the sacraments have the joy of uniting around the Lord in this world so as to participate in his sacrifice and his banquet—the Mass—in expectation of eternal life with him.

To evangelize is to bring this good news to all circles. It is to propose this good news for free adherence by peaceful means and, through its impact, to transform from within, to renew humanity itself.

Belief in the Infallibility of the Church Is Belief in the Gift of Christ

Belief in the power of the Church is not belief in the power of men who constitute her but belief in the gift of Christ: in that power which—as St. Paul says—"is manifested fully in weakness" (2 Cor 12:9).

Belief in the holiness of the Church is not belief in the natural perfection of man but belief in the gift of Christ: in that gift which makes us who are heirs of sin into heirs of the divine holiness.

Belief in the infallibility of the Church is not, in any way, belief in the infallibility of man, but belief in the gift of Christ: in that gift which enables fallible men to proclaim infallibly and confess infallibly the truth revealed for our salvation.

The Church of our day—of this difficult and perilous age in which we live, this critical age—must have a particular certainty about the gift of Christ, the gift of power, the gift of holiness, the gift of infallibility. The more conscious she is of man's weakness, sinfulness, and fallibility, the more must she guard the certainty of those gifts that stem from her Redeemer and Bridegroom.

Life—Proof of Fidelity

God does not want us to be saved and happy in an unconscious way or through force. He requires our conscious and free collaboration, placing us before the "tree of the knowledge of good and evil." Or rather he sets a choice before us and desires a proof of our fidelity.

The Eucharist Signifies, Recalls, and Effects Charity

The Eucharist signifies charity—hence recalls it, makes it present, and effects it at the same time.

Every time we participate in the Eucharist in a conscious way, a real dimension is opened in our soul of that inscrutable love which contains within it all that God has done for men and that he continuously does, in accord with Christ's words.

Eucharistic worship is thus the expression of that love which is the authentic and most profound characteristic of the Christian vocation. This worship arises from and serves that love to which all of us are called in Jesus Christ.

Every Man Is My Brother in Christ

We must become particularly sensitive to all human suffering and misery, to all injustice and wrong, and seek the way to remedy it in an effective manner. Let us learn how to discover with respect the truth about the inner man, so that this interior of man may become the dwelling of God who is present in the Eucharist. Christ comes into the hearts of our brothers and sisters and visits their consciences. What a change comes over the image of all and each of them when we become aware of this reality, when we make it the object of our reflection! The meaning of the eucharistic mystery spurs us on to love for our neighbor, for all men.

Knowing How to Suffer with the Suffering

Suffering is in our midst, near us, in the very buildings we inhabit, possibly hidden under a veil of reserve that is ashamed to ask.

Our daily work must not only refrain from blunting the spiritual eye against discovering the pains and privations of others but in fact must sharpen it, heighten its sensitivity, and stir up "sympathy," that is, the ability "to suffer with another."

The Pilgrim's Walking Stick and the Rights of Man

A more real observance and "implementation" of the totality of man's rights are precisely the objectives that cause me to frequently take up the pilgrim's walking stick in order to awaken or reawaken the conscience of humanity. It is a question of man's greatness.

It is by this that man will assert himself rather than by the chase after illusory and futile power. Man has a particular right to peace and security. He has a right that the state—responsible for the common good—should teach him to practice the means of peace.

The Church has always taught, as I have set down in my encyclical "The Redeemer of Man," that "the fundamental duty of power is solicitude for the common good of society. . . . In the name of these premises of the objective ethical order, the rights of power can only be understood on the basis of respect for the objective and inviolable rights of man. . . . The lack of this leads to the dissolution of society, opposition by citizens to authority, or a situation of oppression, intimidation, violence, and terrorism, of which many examples have been provided by the totalitarianisms of this century."

Christ Has Become Poor to Enrich Us by His Poverty

I will simply recall a few words of our Lord that should fill us with joy and hope. As a sign that God has truly come down among men, he has said: "The poor accept the Gospel," the poor understand the good news of salvation!

He has also said: "Come to me, all you who are weighed down by a heavy yoke, and I will refresh you." I wish to recall for all of Christ's followers this sublime message of the Gospel that is at the basis of the love we feel for one another, and I recall what Paul taught the first Christians: "The Lord Jesus made himself poor for us, and enriched us with his poverty." This is realized even today.

Men Are Only Managers of Creation

The Christian churches do not have to propose, nor do they have to realize, technical solutions for the leasing of the rural world. But they are custodians of the evangelical meaning to be given to the life of human beings and societies.

Christians formed by them will bring to these human

solutions a dimension that will illumine the choice of objectives and methods. They will be, for example, concerned with respect for persons. They will care for the lowly and the weak.

Their honesty will not tolerate corruption. They will seek more just structures in the area of real estate. They will give value to mutual help and solidarity. They will desire to preserve a fraternal appearance for their community. They will be workers for peace. They will regard themselves as managers of God's creation, which must never be wasted or exterminated by one's own will, because it is entrusted to men for the good of all.

They will avoid the affirmation of a materialism that would in fact be a bondage. In short, they want to work from now on for a world more worthy of the children of God. This is the role that the Church recognizes for the Christian laity, aided by their pastors.

JULY 19

Jesus Is the True Simplicity of the Rural Life

For Jesus, in fact, his earthly life unfolded above all in an essentially agricultural civilization. He spent thirty years in one of the smallest villages of Palestine—Nazareth. And during his public life, he visited numerous villages made up of farmers and poor fishermen.

He had long observed and loved nature, the flowers and trees, the seasons, the activities in the fields, those of the worker, the harvester, the vine-dresser, the shepherd, the woman who goes to draw water, who works the yeast, and who prepares the meal.

He took part in village events, the hospitality offered to friends, at weddings, and at mourning.

He paused by children at play and by the sick in their

suffering. We know this because he made marvelous use of all of those observations to help his hearers understand the mysteries of the kingdom of God that he had come to reveal. So true is this that the Gospel is for rural dwellers a book filled with an appealing language that is very understandable to them.

The Way of Man Leads to God

Man is the being who seeks God. Diverse are the ways of this quest and manifold are the histories of human souls along these very paths. At times the ways seem very simple and near. At other times, they are difficult, complicated, and far. At times, man easily arrives at his "eureka": "I have found it." At other times, he struggles with difficulty, as if he could not penetrate himself and the world, and above all as if he could not comprehend the evil that is in the world. We know that even from the context of birth this evil has demonstrated its threatening visage.

Not a few are the men who have described their quest for God along the paths of their lives. Even more numerous are those who remain silent, regarding as the most profound and intimate mystery all that they have lived along these paths: how they have experienced, how they have searched, how they have lost their bearings, and how they have found them anew.

Man is the being who seeks God. And even after finding him, he continues to seek him. And if he seeks him with sincerity, he has already found him—as, in a famous passage from Pascal, Jesus says to man: "Be comforted; you would not be seeking me if you had not already found me."

This is the truth about man. It cannot be falsified. nor can it even be destroyed. It must be left for man so that it may define him.

Work Must Help Man to Be More Human

Work is the fundamental dimension of man's existence on earth. For man, work has not only a technological meaning but also an ethical one. We can say that man subdues the earth when he himself, by his conduct, becomes its master rather than its slave.

Work must help man to become better, spiritually more mature, more responsible, so that he can fulfill his vocation on earth.

Work must help man to become more human. Work, even in its fatiguing, boring, and constraining dimensions—in which we can see the consequences of original sin—was given to man by God, before sin, precisely as a means for the elevation and perfection of the cosmos, as the complement of personality, and as a collaboration in God's creative process.

The effort connected with work associates man with the value of Christ's redeeming cross; and, in the totalizing view of the Gospel, it becomes a means for sociality among brothers, for mutual collaboration, and reciprocal perfecting, already on the plane of earthly life. In a word, it becomes the expression of charity in the unique love of Christ, which should impel us to seek one another's good and bear one another's burdens.

A Life Freed from the Tyranny of Possessing, Consuming, and Dominating

In opposition to the current demagogies, you should encourage the quest for more simple ways of life, less abandoned to the tyrannical thrust of the instincts to possess, consume, and dominate, and more disposed to the profound rhythms of personal creativity and friendship. In this way, you will open up for yourselves and all others an immense area for unsuspected possibilities of peace.

Testimonies of Good and of Love

Every authentic love reproposes in a certain measure the primitive value judgment made by God, repeating with the Creator on encountering every concrete human being that his existence is "something very good."

How can we fail to recall, in this respect, the insistence with which St. Paul returns to the universal dimension of charity? He states that he has been made a slave of all, that he has become "all things for all men"; and he exhorts us: "so long as we have the opportunity, let us do good to all men."

Conjugal Union, an Unrepeatable Gift on the Part of Two Persons

In conjugal "knowledge," the woman "is given" to the man and he to her, since the body and sex enter directly into the very structure and content of this "knowledge."

In this way, therefore, the reality of the conjugal union, in which the man and the woman become "one single flesh," contains in itself a new and, in a certain sense, definitive discovery of the significance of the human body in its masculinity and femininity.

But with respect to this discovery, is it just to speak

only of "sexual sharing"? It must be kept in mind that each of them, man and woman, is not only a passive object, defined by the proper body and sex, and in this way determined by nature. On the contrary, precisely because of the fact of being man and woman, each of them is given to the other as the unique and unrepeatable subject, as an "I," as a person.

Sex Is Something More Than the Mysterious Force of Human Corporeity

By uniting with one another (in the conjugal act) so closely as to become "one single flesh," man and woman rediscover, so to speak, each time and in a special way the mystery of creation. They thus return to that union in humanity ("flesh of my flesh and bone of my bone") which permits them to know each other mutually and, like the first time, to call each other by name.

This signifies that they relive, in a certain sense, the original virginal value of man, who emerges from the mystery of his solitude before God and in the midst of the world. The fact that they become "one single flesh" is a powerful bond established by the Creator, through which they discover their own humanity, whether in its original unity or in the duality of a mysterious mutual attraction.

However, sex is something more than the mysterious force of human corporeity, which acts almost by instinct. At the level of man and in the reciprocal relations of persons, sex expresses an ever new surpassing of the limits of man's solitude inherent in the constitution of his body, and it determines its original meaning.

This surpassing always contains in itself a certain assumption of the solitude of the body of the second "I" as one's own.

Temperance Is Indispensable So That Man May Be Fully Human

The temperate man is the one who is master of himself, the one in whom the passions do not have the upper hand over reason, the will, and even the "heart." The man who knows how to rule over himself! If such is the case, we can easily realize what fundamental and rudimentary value the virtue of temperance possesses. It is absolutely indispensable so that man may be fully human.

The "Specific Weight" of Life

Life is beautiful and has value only if it is spent responsibly in the service of one's brothers.

Never Let Yourselves Be Degraded By Work

Workers, never lose sight of the great nobility that, as men and as Christians, you must imprint on your work, even the most humble and insignificant.

Never let yourselves be degraded by work. Indeed work makes you, first of all, collaborators with God in the continuation of the work of creation.

Bring forward—with the sweat of your brow but above all with the just pride of being created in the image of God himself—the dynamism contained in the command given by God to the first man, to populate the earth and subdue it.

The Man Without God and Without Christ Builds on Sand

The Christian conception of work starts from faith in God the Creator and through Christ the Redeemer arrives at the building up of human society, at the solidarity of all men.

Without this vision, all effort whatever—even the most tenacious—is wanting and fleeting.

It is destined to delude and to fail. The man without God and without Christ builds on sand. He betrays his own origin and nobility. And he ultimately harms man and offends his brother.

How Much Suffering and Misery Are Caused By Unemployment!

How much suffering, how much anguish and misery are caused by unemployment!

Consequently, the first and fundamental concern of all and everyone—government leaders, politicians, syndicate directors, and owners of businesses—must be this: to provide work for all.

To expect the resolution of the problem through the more or less automatic result of a command and an economic development, no matter what it may be, in which employment appears as a secondary consequence, is neither realistic nor admissible.

Unrestrained Luxury and the Frustration of the Disinherited

Many times economic development is transformed into a gigantic version of the parable of the rich man and Lazarus. The proximity of luxury and poverty accentuates the feeling of frustration on the part of the disinherited.

How can we transform the city into a truly human city, in its natural environment, in its constructions, and in its institutions?

An essential condition for doing so is to give the economy a human meaning and logic. We must free the various fields of existence from the domination of a subjugating economism.

† † †

August

Vacation as a Time of Rediscovery and the Possibility of Praise

Vacation time offers so many persons the opportunity for a more direct contact with nature. It is important for each of us to become an attentive observer of the wonders of creation, its ever new beauty, its inexhaustible fecundity, and its suggestive and mysterious profundity.

The rediscovery of these values, from whose charm modern life too often keeps us far away, gives birth in our hearts to a feeling of joyous gratitude that is easily transformed into prayer: "Bless the Lord, O my soul; O Lord, my God, how great you are! Clothed in majesty and splendor, wrapped in light as a cloak. You stretch out the sky like a tent, you construct your dwelling on the waters, you make the clouds your chariot, and you walk on the wings of the wind. . . ."

Vacation as the Occasion for Encountering God

The mountain slopes, the forests, the lakes, and the seashores attract large crowds in the summer. Nevertheless, for many groups of young people this repose that man finds in the heart of nature becomes a particular occasion for closer contact with God. And they rediscover this in the exuberant beauty of nature, which for many souls and many hearts has become, throughout history, a source of religious inspiration.

In this twofold encounter, they rediscover themselves, they rediscover their most proper and profound "I," their innermost self. Nature helps them do so.

The human innermost self becomes, upon contact with nature, transparent to man and more open to deep reflection and the action of grace, which awaits the inner recollection of the youthful heart in order to act with greater efficacy.

AUGUST 3

The Value of Rest

Rest pertains not only to the human order but also to the divine program for human life.

The person rests well who works well and, in turn, the person who works well must rest well.

AUGUST 4

Especially During Vacation Time, Let Us Remember Those Suffering

All around us, in every village, in every city, great or small, in every country, and in every continent, there are people suffering. There are the sick, the gravely ill, the incurable, and the invalids; persons doomed to move with the aid of a wheelchair; women and men chained to a bed of pain.

Possibly it is precisely at this time of the year—when healthy people enjoy a time of rest in the mountains, in the forests, at the seashore, and at the lakeside—that our suffering brothers feel their state more painfully. For them, these simple and legitimate joys of life—the charm of summer, of rest, and of fresh air—are limited, most limited, and even inaccessible.

When we reflect on the immensity of human pain— that pain which is in our midst, in our homes, in hospitals, in clinics, and all over the world—the significance of Christ's words becomes extremely real for us: "Whenever you did these things for the least of my brothers [who were suffering] you did them for me" (Mt 25:40).

How Christ becomes multiplied by these words! How present he is in the history of mankind! And how many people in the world "do something for him" even though they are not aware of it and possibly do not even know that he exists. . . .

AUGUST 5

The True Disciples of Christ Are Workers for Peace

The aspiration for peace corresponds to God's initial call to form a single family of brothers, created in the image of the same Father.

Revelation insists on our freedom and solidarity. The difficulties that we encounter in our journey toward peace are tied in part to our weakness as creatures whose steps are necessarily slow and gradual; they are heightened by our egoisms and our sins of every kind, after that original sin that marked a break with God and determined a break also among brothers.

The image of the tower of Babel gives a good description of the situation. But we believe that Jesus Christ, with the gift of his life on the cross, has become our peace: he has broken down the barrier of hostility that separated brothers (cf. Eph 2:14). Having risen and entered into the glory of the Father, he associates us mysteriously in his life:

reconciling us with God, he heals the wounds of sin and division and makes us capable of inscribing in our societies a sketch of that unity which he reestablishes in us.

The most faithful disciples of Christ have been workers for peace, going so far as to pardon their enemies and even at times to offer their lives for them. Their example traces the path for a new humanity that is no longer content with provisional compromises but realizes the most profound brotherhood.

We Must Work for Peace and Pray for Peace

Peace is our work: it demands on our part a courageous and united action. But peace is at the same time and above all a gift of God: it requires our prayer. Christians must be among the first who pray daily for peace.

Encounter with the World in the Spirit of True Universality

The soul that lives in habitual contact with God and moves within the warm ray of his love knows how to guard without difficulty against the temptation of particularisms and oppositions, which create the risk of painful divisions. Such a soul knows how to interpret in the just light of the Gospel the option for the most poor and for every victim of human egoism. It knows how to do so without yielding to sociopolitical radicalizations, which in the long run turn out to be inopportune and counterproductive, and themselves spawn new oppressions. Such a soul knows how to draw near people and become part of the populace without jeopardizing its own identity.

*The Eucharist Responds to the Various Kinds of Hunger of
Contemporary Man*

The Eucharist—the sacrament of the death and resurrection of Jesus Christ, the sacrament of his Flesh and Blood—is placed at the center of the life of the great human family. It responds fully to the various kinds of hunger of contemporary man.

*The Great Instrument for Bringing Men
Closer to One Another*

The eucharistic communion constitutes the sign of the reunion of all the faithful. It is a truly indicative sign, because at the sacred table all difference of race or social class disappears, leaving only the participation of everyone in the same sacred meal.

This participation, identical in all, signifies and accomplishes the suppression of all that divides men and brings about the meeting of all at a higher level, where every opposition is eliminated.

The Eucharist thus becomes the great instrument for bringing men closer to one another. Each time the faithful participate therein with a sincere heart, they receive a new stimulus to establish a better rapport with others.

God Becomes Converted to Us through the Cross of Christ

Let us open ourselves to God, who wants to open himself to us. Conversion is not a one-sided process. It is an expression of reciprocity. To be converted means to believe in God who has first loved us, who has loved us eternally in his Son, and who through the Son gives us the grace and truth of the Holy Spirit. That Son has been crucified in order to speak to us with his arms opened as wide as God is open to us. How unceasingly, through the cross of his Son, God "converts" himself to us!

In this way, our conversion is not at all a unilateral aspiration. It is not only an effort of the human will, intellect, and heart. It is not only the commitment to direct toward the heights our humanity that tends heavily toward the depths. Conversion is before all else acceptance. It is the effort of accepting God in all the riches of his "conversion" toward man. This conversion is a grace. The effort of the intellect is also indispensable for the acceptance of grace. It is indispensable so as not to lose the divine dimension of life in the human dimension: to persevere in it.

The Words That Have a Transforming Power

The divine economy of salvation—as Christ has revealed—is doubtless manifested by the liberation of man from that evil which is physical suffering. But it is even more clearly manifested by the inner transformation of that evil which is spiritual suffering, by the "salvific" good, by the good which sanctifies the person who is suffering as well as others who are suffering through him. Therefore, the text on which we must dwell above all is not "I will it, be cured," but "Be imitators of me."

It is St. Paul who addresses these words to the Corinthians: "Be imitators of me, as I am of Christ." Before him, Christ himself had said many times: "Come, follow me."

These words do not have the power to heal, nor do

they free from suffering. However, they do have a transforming power. They are a summons to become a new man, to become particularly like Christ in order to find in this likeness, by means of grace, all the inner good in that which is in itself an evil, which is suffering, which is limiting, and which is possibly humiliating or makes one uneasy. And Christ says to the suffering person: "Come, follow me!"

The Church Is Built Up through Communion with the Son of God

The Church was founded, as a new community of the people of God, in the apostolic community of those twelve who during the Last Supper became partakers of the Lord's body and blood under the appearances of bread and wine.

Christ had said to them: "Take and eat . . ., take and drink." And in fulfillment of this command, they entered for the first time into sacramental communion with the Son of God, a communion, which is the pledge of eternal life.

From that moment until the end of the world, the Church is built up through the same communion with the Son of God, which is the pledge of the eternal Easter.

Christians Joyous in Faith

The most precious gift the Church can offer today's disoriented and disquieted world is to form within it Christians who are securely and humbly joyous in their faith.

The person who wants to understand himself to his very depths—not only according to the immediate, partial, often superficial, and even apparent criteria and measurements of his own being—must draw near with all his weakness and sinfulness, with his life and death, to Christ.

He must, so to speak, enter into him with all of himself; he must appropriate to himself and assimilate the whole reality of the incarnation and the redemption in order to find himself.

The Church Is Realized in the Sacrifice of Christ

The Church is realized when in fraternal union we celebrate the sacrifice of the cross of Christ, when we proclaim "the death of the Lord until he comes," and consequently when we are profoundly compenetrated by the mystery of our salvation and draw nourishment in a sacramental way from the fruits of the propitiatory sacrifice.

In eucharistic communion, we thus receive Christ himself; and our union with him, which is a gift and a grace for everyone, brings it about that in him we are also associated in the unity of his body, which is the Church.

Everyone Welcomes Within Himself the Word of God

The words of the Magnificat manifest the whole heart of our mother. They constitute her spiritual testament.

Each of us must regard our own lives and the history of mankind in a certain way with the eyes of Mary

In this respect, the words of St. Ambrose are very beautiful: "Let the soul of Mary be in everyone to magnify the Lord. Let the spirit of Mary be in everyone to exult in the Lord. If, according to the flesh, only one is the mother of Christ, according to the faith all souls generate Christ: for everyone welcomes within him the Word of God."

Procreation Is Rooted in Creation

In every conjugal union of man and woman there is newly discovered the same original awareness of the unitive significance of the body in its masculinity and femininity. The biblical text indicates, at the same time, that in each such union there is renewed in a certain way the mystery of creation in all its original profundity and vital force.

"Taken from man" as "flesh of his flesh," woman goes on to become, as "wife" and in virtue of motherhood, the mother of all the living (Gn 3:20), because her motherhood has its proper origin also in him. Procreation is rooted in creation and in a certain sense always reproduces its mystery.

The Revelation of the New Man

Procreation brings it about that man and woman (his wife) know each other reciprocally in a "third" person, originating from the two of them. Therefore, this "knowledge" becomes a discovery and in a certain sense a revelation of a new man, in whom both of them, man and woman, recognize themselves anew, their humanity and their living image.

"Knowledge" in the biblical sense signifies that man's "biological" determination, on the part of his body and sex, ceases to be something passive and reaches a level and content specific to self-aware and self-determining persons.

Hence, it entails a particular awareness of the meaning of the human body, connected with fatherhood and motherhood.

The Freedom to Make a Gift of Oneself

If Christ has revealed to man and woman, over and above the vocation of marriage, another vocation—that is, the vocation to renounce marriage in view of the kingdom of heaven—he has with this vocation emphasized the same truth about the human person.

If man and woman are capable of making a gift of themselves for the kingdom of heaven, this proves in its turn (and possibly even more) that there is the freedom to give in the human body. This means that the body possesses a full "nuptial" significance.

The Option of Love

I set before you the option of love which is the opposite of flight. If you really accept the love that comes from Christ, it will lead you to God.

Whatever you make of your life, make sure that it is a reflection of Christ's love.

The whole people of God will be enriched by the diversity of your commitments.

In everything you do, remember that Christ calls you, in one way or another, to a service of love. Love for God and neighbor.

Accepting Christ's Message Without Reductions of Convenience

There is need of a coherent and courageous testimony of faith. In this sense, St. Paul, writing to the Ephesians, sets forth a program of life.

We must first of all abandon the worldly and pagan mentality: "I solemnly attest in the Lord that you must no longer live as the pagans do, in the emptiness of their minds."

Then we must transform the worldly and terrestrial mentality into the mentality of Christ: "You must lay aside the old man with the former way of life, the old self which deteriorates through deceptive passions."

Finally, we must accept the whole message of Christ without reductions of convenience and in accord with his example: "You must be renewed in the spirit of your minds and put on the new man, created according to God in justice and true holiness" (Eph 4:17, 20–24).

This is a very demanding program, which under certain aspects could even be termed heroic. Yet we must present it to ourselves and to others in its integralness, relying on the action of grace, which can give to each of us the generosity to accept the responsibility for our own actions in terms of eternity and for the good of society.

The Definition of the Christian Corresponds to the Definition of Man

To be a Christian means to be a witness to Christ.

This is a fundamental tradition of the Church. In her foundations there is precisely this bearing witness. The course of her existence is strewn with witnesses: not only in the first three centuries, the centuries of bloody persecutions but also in the succeeding centuries, including our own times.

This is a magnificent truth about the Christian life. But this truth about the Christian life, this definition of the Christian, corresponds profoundly even with the definition of man. Man is himself because he relates himself to the truth, aspires to the truth, and seeks to know it. And, when he knows it, when he has recognized it, he becomes converted to it, works in accord with it, and testifies to it in his social life.

Without this attitude toward the truth, man does not realize his humanity. He remains ill-defined, vague, and inexpressive.

Without God, What Remains of Man?

We live in times when God is forgotten, when God is not acknowledged, when God is stricken from publications, books, and programs of public life. It is a world deprived of God, deprived of its beginning and its end, a world snatched away from its Creator. This is the image, this is the ideology, that is sought to be inculcated by various ways in man: a world without God.

Yet precisely from all of these projects there arises our need for an encounter with Christ who says: "I acknowledge you, Father, Lord of heaven and earth."

The need to proclaim God is a sign peculiar to the times in which we live, the times in which some strive to delete the name of God, seeking to do so at the very depths of the human soul.

This is a terrible thing from the viewpoint of our Christian sense of reality. God indeed signifies Creator and

Father. If we separate ourselves from the Creator and cancel God, what remains of the creature? What remains of man?

Strong and Courageous for a New World

We cannot think of building a new world without being strong and courageous in overcoming the false ideas in vogue, the world's criteria of violence, and the suggestions of evil.

All of this demands that we topple the barriers of fear in order to give our witness to Christ and offer at the same time—the two realities are superimposed on each other—an image of the true man, who is expressed uniquely in love, in giving of self.

Christians in the Name and in the Mystery of Christ

Christians are those who have received the name of Christ; those who bear his mystery within them; those who belong to him with all their humanity; those who, with full awareness and freedom, "consent that he imprint on their human existence the dignity of children of God." Christians!

Original Innocence

If creation is a gift to man, then its fullness and its most profound dimension are determined by grace, that is, by participation in the inner life of God himself, in his holiness. In man, this is also the interior foundation and source of his original innocence.

The Love of God Impels Christians to Reacquire Unity

Faith has its beginning in the Word of God, in the Gospel, in the testimony of Jesus Christ, Son of God.

If this faith and its content have in the course of time created different forms in the minds of followers, of men, there is the need to seek the way to achieve a unity of faith. Only such a quest brings us close together; it alone makes us cease to be strangers and draws us close together on the most essential questions!

This energy and this creative search for unity arise from no other source than that of love. "The love of God has been poured forth in our hearts by the Holy Spirit." By means of love, therefore, we seek the path toward one another, and this signifies that we are no longer strangers.

We Are the Voice of All Creation

Man must give glory to God the Creator and Redeemer; he must, in some way, become the voice of all creation to say in its name: "Magnificat." He must proclaim the "magnalia Dei," the wondrous works of God, and, at the same time, express himself in this sublime relation with God, because in the visible world he alone can do so.

Prayer, Our Continuous Conversion

When Christ—in reply to the request of his disciples, "Teach us to pray"—pronounces the words of his prayer, he not only teaches the words but also teaches that in our colloquy with the Father there must be total sincerity and complete openness.

Prayer must embrace all that constitutes the parts of our lives. It cannot be something supplementary or marginal. Everything must find in prayer its own voice. Even everything that irritates us; everything that we are ashamed of; everything that by its nature separates us from God. Precisely this above all. It is prayer that always, first and essentially, tears down the barrier between us and God that sin and evil may have erected.

By means of prayer, the whole world must find its just reference: that is, the reference to God: my inner world and also the objective world, the one that we live in and the one that we know. If we become converted to God, everything in us is oriented toward him. Prayer is the expression of this orientation toward God; and this is at the same time our continuous conversion.

Prayer, a Profoundly Demanding Gift

Prayer is an invisible bond that unites the community of the faithful. It is a very powerful and very profound bond. In it is expressed the spiritual unity of the people of God.

The gift of prayer is a particular gift. It is a profoundly demanding gift.

It is the source of continuous strengthening. Christ,

who has recommended to Peter: "Confirm your brothers" (Lk 22:32), based this recommendation on his own prayer. He said: "I have prayed for you, that your faith may not fail" (Lk 22:32). And when the difficult moment arrived, he gave Peter that strengthening about which we read in the Acts of the Apostles: the Church prayed for Peter.

This great service cannot be exercised diversely except on the basis of profound certitude of faith, stemming from the words of Christ directed once to Peter and, at the same time, on the basis of the prayer of the whole Church.

For this prayer, I wish today to thank all and every one in particular.

Let all remember that I think about them as my benefactors.

Sunday, Day of the Eucharistic Community

From early Christian times, from the times of the Apostles, Sunday has been the day of the eucharistic community.

On this day we recall the mystery of death and resurrection, and Christians receive this sacramental remembrance in which Christ left the mystery of his death and resurrection, the mystery of himself, so that he might be the food of souls.

This is what Sunday means in the life of a Christian family.

The Magic of Being Young

To be young means to live in oneself an increasing newness of spirit, to foster a continuous quest for good, to emit an impulse to transform oneself ever for the better, and to experience a persevering will for giving.

Who will grant us all of this? Has man in himself the strength to confront with his own forces the snares of evil, of egotism, and—let us say it clearly—the snares of the "prince of this world," who is ever working first to give man a false sense of his autonomies and then to lead him through failure into the precipice of desperation?

All of us, both young people and adults, must have recourse to Christ eternally young, to Christ conqueror of every expression of death, to Christ risen forever, to Christ who in the Holy Spirit communicates the continuous eruptive life of the Father. And we must do so with the purpose of establishing and ensuring the hope for the tomorrow, which you will build, but which is already potentially present in "today."

† † †

September

Grafting Good, the Work of Catechesis

The catechesis of children and young people tends everywhere and always to increase in youthful souls what is good, noble, and worthy.

It becomes an education in the better and more mature sense of humanity, which is developed upon contact with Christ.

There is, in fact, no more effective instrument for protecting from scandal and for extricating oneself from evil, from demoralization, from the sense of the futility of life, and from frustration than the instrument of grafting on good, infusing it deeply and vigorously into young souls.

Vigilance that such good may flower and mature pertains to the formative function of catechesis.

We Must Make Every Task a Masterpiece of Love and Perfection

Matthew the evangelist narrates that "Jesus called a child to him, placed him in their midst, and said: 'Truly, I say to you: Unless you are converted and become like little children, you will not enter the kingdom of heaven. Therefore, whoever makes himself lowly like this child is the greatest in the kingdom of heaven' " (Mt 18:2–4).

Jesus does not wish to oblige the Christian to remain in a situation of perpetual infantilism, of complacent ignorance, and of insensitivity to the problems of the age. Just the opposite! However, he holds up the child as an exemplar for entering the kingdom of heaven because of the symbolic value that the child carries within him.

First of all, the child is innocent, and to enter the kingdom of heaven the primary requisite is the life of "grace," that is, innocence whether preserved or reacquired, the exclusion of sin, which is always an act of pride and egotism.

Secondly, the child lives by faith and trust in his parents, and entrusts himself completely to those who guide him and love him. Similarly, the Christian must be humble and entrust himself with complete confidence to Christ and the Church. The great danger and the great enemy is ever pride, and if Jesus insists on the virtue of humility it is because one can be nothing but humble in the face of the infinite. Humility is truth, and it is also the mark of intelligence and the source of serenity.

Finally, the child is satisfied with little things, which suffice to make him happy: any small success, any deserved good wishes, or any word of praise is enough to make him exult with joy.

To enter the kingdom of heaven we must have sublime, immense, and universal sentiments. But we must also know how to be satisfied with little things, with obligations dictated by obedience, with the will of God as expressed in the moments that fly by, and with the daily joys offered by Providence. We must make every task, no matter how hidden and modest, a masterpiece of love and perfection.

In Children Lies the World's Tomorrow

Christ attributed an enormous importance to the child. He made him, as it were, the spokesman for the cause that he proclaimed and for which he gave his life. He made him the representative, the most simple, of that cause, a veritable prophet for it.

The value of the child in any society lies in the fact that he bears witness to the innocence conceived for man by the Creator and heavenly Father.

Lost through sin, this innocence must be reacquired by each of us at the cost of effort. In this effort, in this endeavor of the mind, the will, and the heart, the image of the child constitutes inspiration and a source of hope for man. God, who as a father calls us all to our true home, will help us to recover the innocence of the child.

The child is a source of hope. He speaks to his parents of the purpose of their life, and he represents the fruit of their love. In addition, he allows them to think of the future. Parents live for their children; they work and toil for them. And not only in families but also in every society, the child is a reminder of the future. In children the nation sees its own tomorrow, just as the Church sees in them her own tomorrow.

Christ's Message Does Not Allow Adulteration

We must never be afraid of setting forth Christ's message in all its evangelical purity, because, as I have said on another occasion: "We are never afraid that the obligation will be too great for our people. It has been redeemed by the precious blood of Christ and is his people."

Through the Holy Spirit, Jesus Christ reserves for himself the ultimate responsibility for the acceptance of his word and consequently for the growth of his Church. It is he, Jesus Christ, who will continue to give his people the grace to face the demands of his word, in spite of all difficulties and every weakness. And it is for us to continue to proclaim the message of salvation in its integrity and purity, with patience and compassion, convinced that what is impossible to man is possible to God.

Man, the Basis of All Things

Man is the basis of all things. He must be respected in his personal and transcendent dignity.

His social dimension must be respected: the human and Christian personality cannot realize itself, in fact, except to the extent that exclusivistic egotism is rejected, because man's call is at once personal and social.

Clarity of Ideals in Order to Protect Civil Life in Common

In order to protect civil life in common from all subverting and destructive impulses, it is necessary to return without delay to a clarity of ideals, to a certainty of emblematic values, and to the interpretation of man and his destiny offered by the Gospel and the law of God.

Without a common effort to form man, it is useless to think of being able to safeguard the coefficients of true prosperity and genuine progress.

Constantly animated by proposals of respect for the dignity of human life, magnanimous dedication to duty, impartial protection of legality, and courageous defense of the rights of citizens, especially the most weak and defenseless, you will gain the esteem of all persons of good will—and this includes almost everybody—who aspire to and labor for a free and democratic native land, harmoniously looking toward the conquest of ever more advanced goals of honest and fraternal life together, solidarity and peace.

Missionaries of Certitude

A great ideological confusion engulfs the minds of people, leading to the denial of transcendence or its confinement to a vague mysticism of an emotional nature. As a result, people speak of a radical crisis of all values, and there follows a dramatic situation of social unrest, pedagogical insecurity, uncertainty, intolerance, fear, violence, and neuroses.

In the midst of such a situation, Christ says to you as he said to the apostles: "Do not be afraid of men" (Mt 10:26; Lk 12:4); "I will be with you until the end of the world" (Mt 28:20).

In an afflicted world, tormented by so many doubts and so much anguish, you must be missionaries of certitude;

—certitude about transcendent values, reached through the good and wholesome philosophy that was rightly termed "perennial," in the footsteps of the Angelic Doctor, St. Thomas, while integrating it with the contributions of modern thought;

—certitude about the person of Christ, true man and true God, historic and definitive manifestation of God to humanity, through his inner illumination and his redemption;

—certitude about the historical reality and divine mission of the Church, expressly willed by Christ for the transmission of the revealed doctrine and the means of sanctification and salvation.

The Courage to Be Open to Others

The vocation of the Christian is realized substantially not only in the life of grace but also in the testimony of love and solidarity, which obviously requires an openness to others, accepted as they are, and strains to emerge from oneself, from one's fears and defenses, from the tranquillity of one's well-being, to communicate and at the same time to construct a network of reciprocal relations, directed to the spiritual, moral, and social good of all.

The Church Will Always Lift Up Her Voice on Behalf of the Dignity of the Whole Person

I wish to repeat that the Church is deeply interested in all the needs of the people. Precisely because she has the greatest esteem for the dignity of every human being, she will always continue to carry out her mission, in accord with her proper nature, for the genuine good of man and society and for the benefit of the whole human person.

In this spirit, the Church contributes to the development, unity, fraternity, and peace among peoples and among nations. For this reason, the Church will raise her voice and rally her sons and daughters whenever the life conditions of persons and communities are not truly human; whenever they are not in harmony with human dignity.

Characteristics of Love

Love is realized in the most profound way when the person desires to cease belonging exclusively to himself so as to belong also to others. He renounces being independent and inalienable.

Love passes through this renunciation, guided by the deep conviction that it leads not to a diminishment or impoverishment but on the contrary to an enrichment and an increase of a person's being. It is a kind of law of "ecstasy": to go out of self in order to find in others an increase of being (in no other form of love is this law applied with such evidence as it is in conjugal love).

Whereas purely emotional love is characterized by an idealization of its object, love that is based on value of the person ensures that we will love him as he really is—not our idea of him but the real being. We love him with his virtues and his defects, and up to a certain point independently of his virtues and despite his defects.

The Miracle of Miracles

One thing is sure: the more your love is pure and generous, the more will there shine forth the beauty of Christianity and, as it were, the attractiveness of the Gospel. And the world today has need of this: that is, to see the miracle of miracles, or to show concern for the needy in the most disinterested way, to put to rout egotistical individualism; in the most complete way, in order to overcome the wretched partialities of calculation and opportunism; in the most concrete way, in order not to limit oneself to the sterility of good intentions and fine words; and also in the most hidden, and, I might say, almost modest, way, in order not to depreciate the sincerity of one's gift of self by ostentation, of which others can be masters but certainly not the disciples of Jesus.

The Family Is the Place in Which the Gospel Is Lived and Radiated

The Christian family is also the domestic sanctuary of the Church. In a Christian family are found diverse aspects of the Church in its totality, such as mutual love, attentiveness to the Word of God, and common prayer. The home is the place in which the Gospel is received and lived, and from which it is radiated.

In addition, the family renders daily and even tacit testimony to the truth and to the grace of the Word of God. For this reason I have stated in my encyclical: "Married people . . . must endeavor with all their strength to persevere in their matrimonial union, building up the family community through this witness of love and educating new generations of men and women, capable in their turn of dedicating the whole of their lives to their vocation, that is to say, to the 'kingly service' of which Jesus Christ has offered us the example and the most beautiful model."

The Prayer of the Family Transforms the World

Every effort to make our society sensitive to the importance of the family constitutes a great service rendered to humanity. When the full dignity of parents and children is lived and expressed in prayer, a new energy of good is set loose in the Church and in the world.

John Paul I eloquently expressed this reality when he stated: "The holiness of the Christian family is certainly the most suitable means for producing that serene renewal of the Church which the Council so ardently desires." Thanks to the prayer of the family, the "domestic Church" becomes an effective reality and contributes to the transformation of the world.

SEPTEMBER 14

Progress and Peace

There is no [real] human progress when everything conspires to give full reign to the instincts of self-interest, sex, and power.

We must find a simple way of living. For it is not right that the standard of living of the rich countries should seek to maintain itself by draining off a greater part of the reserves of energy and raw materials that are meant to serve the whole of humanity.

For readiness to create a greater and more equitable solidarity between peoples is the first condition for peace.

SEPTEMBER 15

A Concerted Effort for Peace, Justice, and Moral Values

I desire to do everything possible to solidify the spiritual bonds between Christians and Moslems. Prayer, almsgiving, and fasting are held in high esteem by both our traditions and without doubt constitute a splendid witness for the world which runs the risk of being swallowed up by materialism.

Our relation of reciprocal esteem and the mutual desire for authentic service of mankind free us for a concerted commitment to promote peace, social justice, moral values, and all of the true freedoms of man.

Church and State Side By Side for the Dignity of Man

Respect for human dignity, for the dignity of every man, woman, and child, for the dignity that all human beings possess not because it has been conferred on them by other human beings but because they have received it from God—this is the fundamental attitude to be adopted if we wish to give life to an authentic progress.

It is precisely in this conviction and in this commitment for the dignity of every human person that the Church and the state find themselves on the same path.

A Voluntary Service of Charity

It will be helpful to urge the Christian community to question itself about its charitable presence with regard to the historical evolution of needs and to the emerging request on the part of the new forms of poverty. In this way, it will be possible to individualize the paths that it is necessary to traverse today in order to bear witness in credible terms to the love of God for men, especially the most poor.

It will be necessary to open, above all to youth, the perspectives for a voluntary service of charity, which in place of dispersive and provisional spontaneity substitutes the functionality and continuity of a rational organization of service, understood not only as simple satisfaction of immediate needs but much more as the commitment directed toward modifying the causes that stand at the origin of such needs.

The volunteers opportunely formed will be the natural animators of a process of responsibility on the part of the community, from which they can derive the revision of established structures, the promotion of more just laws, and the creation of more satisfying human relationships.

The Bread That We Need Is the Word of God and Grace

The bread that we need is the Word of God, because "not by bread alone does man live, but by every word that comes from the mouth of God" (Mt 4:4; cf. Dt 8:3).

Doubtless, even men can pronounce words of sublime value. But history shows how the words of men are at times inadequate, ambiguous, deluding, and tendentious; whereas the Word of God is full of truth (cf. 2 Sm 7:28; 1 Cor 17:26); is correct (Ps 33:4); is stable and remains for eternity (cf. Ps 119:89; 1 Pt 1:25).

We must place ourselves continuously in religious reception of such a word, assume it as the criterion of our way of thinking and acting, and get to know it through assiduous reading and personal meditation. But we must above all make it our own, carry it out day by day in our every behavior.

The bread that we need is grace; and we must ask for it. Request it with sincere humility and unwearying constancy, well aware that it is the most precious thing we can possess.

An Undertaking That Is Not Simple Although Not Impossible

It is necessary to escape from the narrow limits of egotism and question our life-style to see in what way it fails to respond to God's call to help us live in the unique human family to which we all belong. We must also grasp the spiritual and material needs of our brothers, who seek our assistance and our help all over the world.

This undertaking is not simple, but with the power of Christ it is not impossible.

Do Not Be Afraid of Christ!

Do not be afraid to welcome Christ and to accept his power! Help the Pope and all those who want to serve Christ and, with the power of Christ, want to serve man and all of humanity!

Do not be afraid! Open—indeed, fling wide—the doors to Christ! Throw open to his saving power the boundaries of states, economic as well as political systems, and the vast fields of culture, civilization, and development.

Do not be afraid! Christ knows "what is in man." He alone knows it! So often, nowadays, man does not know what he carries within himself, in the depths of his spirit, in his heart. Accordingly, he is frequently uncertain of the meaning of his life on this earth. He is invaded by doubt that becomes transformed into despair. I beg you, therefore, and I implore you with humility and confidence—allow Christ to speak to men. He alone has the words of eternal life.

A Heart Open to the Sufferings, Projects, and Joys of Those Around Us

Be very attentive to those who are around you, with charity and always with respect. In parishes, which remain the vital centers of the Christian life; in small neighborhood communities; in scholastic or professional circles—let there enter into your minds and hearts the problems, sufferings, projects, and joys of those who have need of confiding in you, of finding in you moral and spiritual support.

The Easy Yoke of the Lord

The Lord's power—absolute but also gentle and pleasant—responds to the whole depths of man, to his most sublime aspiration of the mind, will, and heart.

It does not speak with a language of force but expresses itself in charity and truth.

Truth Must Flower from Each of Us

"Truth will flourish from the earth."
Indeed, truth must flower from each of us; from
    every heart.
Be faithful to the truth.
Faithful to your vocation.
Faithful to your commitment.
Faithful to your choice.
Be faithful to Christ, who sets free and unites.

Involvement in the World in Order to Transform It

When Pilate asked Jesus if he was a king, our Lord's reply was clear and unambiguous: "My kingdom is not of this world" (Jn 18:35). Christ came to bring life and salvation to every human being: his mission was not of the social, economic, or political order.

Similarly, Christ did not confer on the Church a social, economic, or political mission but a religious one. Yet it would be completely erroneous to believe that individually the Christian should not be involved in these sectors of social life.

In this respect, the fathers of the Second Vatican Council were explicit: "The separation that is verified in many between the faith they profess and the daily life they lead is counted as among the most serious of our time. . . . The Christian who neglects his temporal obligations neglects his duties toward his neighbor, and indeed toward God, and places his eternal salvation in jeopardy."

Therefore, Christians—and especially members of the laity—are called by God to become involved in the world in order to transform it in accord with the Gospel.

Political Life, Great Challenge for the Christian

An important challenge for the Christian is that of political life. In the heart of the state, citizens have the right and the duty to participate in political life. For a nation is able to ensure the common good of all, the dreams and aspirations of its diverse members, only if all of its citizens, with complete freedom and full responsibility, make their proper voluntary and disinterested contribution for the good of all.

The duties of good Christian citizens entail much more than flight from corruption and much more than refraining from exploiting others. Their duties entail the contribution to the establishment of just laws and structures which take account of human values.

If Christians fall into injustice or into anything else that goes counter to love, peace, and unity in society, they must ask themselves: "Where have I failed? What have I done wrong? What have I neglected to do? Have I sinned by omission?"

There Is No Culture in Opposition to God

We must keep in mind that the culture of every generation is created according to the profound laws of the human spirit: mind, heart, and will. It cannot be created artificially; it cannot be created in alienation with all that man thinks and feels, in alienation with all that allows man to express himself, or with all that man lives from.

Culture cannot be created outside of man, and it cannot be created in opposition to man.

Neither can it be created in opposition to God! A culture cannot be created in opposition to the God in whom man believes, the God to whom man confesses, and the God by whom man lives.

Culture cannot be created in opposition to God, because it would then be opposed to man.

The Church Is at Home in Every Culture

One of the sectors that holds great importance in society and in the global vocation of every human person is that of culture: "It is a fact bearing on the very person of man that he can come to an authentic and full humanity only through culture, that is, through the cultivation of natural goods and values. Wherever human life is involved, therefore, nature and culture are quite intimately connected" (GS, no. 53).

A Christian will joyously collaborate in promoting true culture, because he knows that the Good News of Christ reinforces in man the spiritual values that are at the heart of the culture of every people and every historical period.

The Church, which is at home in every culture without exclusively appropriating any particular one, encourages her sons and daughters who work in schools, universities, and other institutions of learning to give them the best of their particular activity.

Harmonizing those values that constitute the unique inheritance of every people or group with the content of the Gospel, the Christian will assist each particular people to attain true freedom and the capacity to face the challenge of its time.

The Importance of Joy

The "beauty of joy" is as important for man as the "beauty of love."

Love Gives Rise to Dialogue

Love is the power that gives rise to dialogue, in which we listen to one another and learn from one another.

Love gives rise, above all, to the dialogue of prayer in

which we listen to God's word, which is alive in the Holy Bible and alive in the life of the Church.

Let love then build the bridges across our differences and at times our contrasting positions. No one in the ecclesial community should ever feel alienated or unloved, even when tensions arise in the course of the common efforts to bring the fruits of the Gospel to society around us.

The Real Poor Are Distinguished by Dignity, Magnanimity, and Openness of Heart

None of us is permitted to reduce himself and his family to wretchedness. We must do all that is licit to ensure for ourselves and our dear ones the necessities of life and sustenance.

In poverty, we must safeguard above all that human dignity and also that magnanimity, that openness of heart to others, and that availability by which the poor in spirit are specifically distinguished.

✝ ✝ ✝

October

Availability Before God

We must always keep in mind that a "Marian" attitude of absolute and docile availability before God is basic to the life of Christians.

This signifies that we must acknowledge—and not only in the abstract—the "primacy of the spiritual," the preeminent value of the interior life, the irreplaceable necessity of union with Jesus Christ, through assiduous prayer, and the constant reception of the sacraments of the Eucharist and reconciliation—which are all conditions for an authentic fecundity in apostolic action, according to the very words of Jesus: "Remain in me and I in you. . . . Whoever remains in me and I in him bears much fruit, because without me you can do nothing. . . . Remain in my love" (Jn 15:4; 5:9).

Nevertheless, the Gospel, the whole Gospel, with its affirmations and demands that are often paradoxical to the current mentality, must animate the life of every Christian, but especially of those who desire to remain faithful to personal commitments for the coming of Christ's kingdom, and be witnesses and broadcasters of it in their circles.

You Pay for Freedom with All of Yourself

Freedom is a continuous conquest that cannot be merely possessed! Its coming is a gift, but to preserve it requires a struggle. Gift and struggle are both written in secret yet patent papers.

You pay for freedom with all of yourself—therefore, you will call freedom that which, although you pay for it, helps you to possess yourself ever anew.

At this cost, we enter into history and touch its epochs.

Where is the watershed between the one who has not paid enough and the one who has paid too much? And to which one do we belong?

Where Is Pilgrim Man Going
Along the Road of the World and of History?

"Where are you going?" Toward what horizons are you turning your efforts, those with which you are laboriously building your future? What goals do you hope to attain through the struggles, the labor, the sacrifices to which you put yourself in your daily lives? Where is pilgrim man going along the road of the world and of history?

Such questions arouse courageous or hesitant, hopeful or sorrowful responses. . . . I believe that if we paid attention to them we would be surprised by the substantial identity existing among [all men]. The paths of men are often very far from meeting. Immediate objectives which they set for themselves normally present characteristics that are not only divergent but often even contrary to each other as well.

However, in the end, the goal to which all head without distinction is always the same. . . . Our heart seeks happiness and would experience it within the texture of a true love. The Christian knows that the authentic satisfaction of this aspiration is to be found only in God, in whose image man was created.

Maturity Is Above All Love

Maturity is also fear,
the whole final harvest is contained in the beginning
and the beginning of wisdom is fear—
but now it rests on other layers of the same soil,
and is no longer an impulse to flee;
it is the space on which greatness is measured.
We penetrate this space
and are ever farther from the beginning
and thus slowly we return:
maturity is above all love,
by which fear is transfigured.

The Martyrology of the Church of Our Day

We cannot forget those who in the course of our age
have suffered death for the faith and for the love of Christ;
who in diverse ways have been imprisoned, tortured, and
condemned to death; and even mocked, deprecated, humiliated, and socially ostracized.

We cannot forget the "martyrology" of the Church
and of the Christians of our day. This martyrology is written with events that differ from those of primitive times.
The methods of martyrdom and bearing witness are different today; but all stem from the same cross of Christ and
complete the same cross of our redemption.

"Crux fidelis . . ." ["O faithful cross . . ."].

The Cross, Response for Every Question of Man to God

Throughout all of the generations of men there will remain this cross, without being separated from Christ. It will become his remembrance and his sign. It will become a response to the question put to God by man, and it will remain a mystery.

The Church will encircle it with the body of her living community, and encircle it with the faith of men, with their hope, and with their love.

The Church will carry the cross with Christ through all generations. She will bear witness to it. She will attain life by it. She will grow from the cross with that mysterious growth of the Spirit which has its beginning in the cross.

The Witness of the Church of Silence

People who live in conditions of freedom and well-being cannot turn their eyes away from the cross and let pass in silence the testimony of those who belong to what is customarily termed "the Church of silence."

The Church, forced into silence under conditions of compulsory atheization, grows ultimately from the cross of Christ. In her silence, she proclaims the greatest truth—the very truth that God has inscribed on the foundations of our redemption.

True Mercy Is the Most Profound Source of Justice

The way that Christ showed us in the Sermon on the Mount with the beatitude regarding those who are merciful is much richer than what we sometimes find in ordinary human opinions about mercy. These opinions see mercy as a unilateral act or process, presupposing and maintaining a certain distance between the one who practices mercy and the one who benefits from it, between the one who does good and the one who receives it. Hence the attempt to free interpersonal and social relationships from mercy and to base them solely on justice.

However, such opinions about mercy fail to see the fundamental link between mercy and justice spoken of by the whole biblical tradition, and above all by the messianic mission of Jesus Christ. True mercy is, so to speak, the most profound source of justice. If justice is in itself suitable for "arbitration" between people concerning the reciprocal distribution of objective goods in an equitable manner, love and only love (including that kindly love that we call "mercy") is capable of restoring man to himself.

Materialism Is a Slavery from Which Man Must Be Protected

I esteem those who endeavor to carry out their existence and to build their city in a vital relationship with God, taking account of the moral exigencies written in the conscience of each one and consequently even the fundamental rights of which God is the guarantor.

I share with those who have this spiritual vision of

man the conviction that materialism, no matter what its source, is a slavery from which man must be protected.

It Cannot Be Man for the System But the System for Man

Justice is the fundamental principle of the existence and coexistence of men, as well as of human communities, societies, and peoples. In addition, justice is the principle of existence of the Church as the people of God, and the principle of coexistence of the Church and the various social structures, especially the state and international organizations.

In this ample and differentiated terrain, man and humanity continually seek justice: this is a perennial process, and it is a task of supreme importance.

We must look with respect on the multiple programs and the activities—at times reformatory—of various tendencies and systems. We must at the same time be aware that it is not a question here primarily of systems but of justice and man. It cannot be man for the system but the system for man. Therefore, we must defend ourselves from the rigidity of the system.

I am thinking of social, economic, political, and cultural systems. They must be sensitive to man, to his integral good. They must be capable of reforming themselves and their very structures in accord with what is demanded by the full truth about man.

The Many Ways of Being Unjust

To be just means to give everyone what is due him. This has to do with temporal goods of a material nature.

The best example can be remuneration for work, or the so-called right to the fruits of one's labor, or to the earth itself. However, man is due also his good name, respect, consideration, and the reputation he has earned.

The more we know a person, the more he reveals to us his personality, his character, his mind, and his heart. And the more we render account to ourselves—and we must render account!—with what criterion "to measure" him and what is meant by being just toward him.

Therefore, we must continually deepen the knowledge of justice. It is not a theoretical science. It is a virtue; it is a capacity of the human spirit, of the human will as well as the heart. We must also pray to be just and to know how to be just.

Many Are Missing Around the Altar

The Church has her principal manifestation in uniting all of her children around the same altar for the celebration of the Eucharist. . . .

The more we find ourselves as brothers and sisters around the charity of Christ, the more grieved we are to see that not all are present to participate in the great mystery.

Freedom Cannot Exist Without Reference to God

The Catholic Church believes that freedom cannot exist and fraternal love is not possible without reference to God, who "created man in his image" (Gn 1:27); she never ceases to defend, as the basic right of every person, freedom of religion and freedom of conscience.

"The curtailment of the religious freedom of individuals and communities is not only a painful experience," I wrote in my [first] encyclical, "but it is above all an attack on man's very dignity, independently of the religion professed or the concept of the world which these individuals and communities have."

I went on to add that, since unbelief, irreligiousness, and atheism can be understood only in relation to the phenomenon of religion and faith, it is difficult to accept "a position that gives only atheism the right to citizenship in public and social life, while believers are, as though by principle, barely tolerated or are treated as second-class citizens or are even—and this has already happened—entirely deprived of the rights of citizenship."

For this reason, the Church believes—without hesitation and without doubt—that an atheistic ideology cannot be the moving and guiding force for an advance of the well-being of persons or for the promotion of social justice when it deprives man of the freedom given by God, of his spiritual inspiration, and of his power to love his neighbor adequately.

OCTOBER 14

Christ Speaks to Us with the Power of His Sacrifice

In the eucharistic liturgy, Christ speaks to us above all with the power of his sacrifice. It is a very concise and ardent discourse. We can say that we know this discourse by heart; yet it always presents itself to us as new, sacred, and revelatory. It contains in itself the whole mystery of love and truth.

God, who is truth and love, has manifested himself in the history of creation and in the history of salvation. He sets forth this history once again by means of this redemptive sacrifice which he has transmitted to us in the sacramental sign, so that not only may we think about it again in remembrance, but we may also renew and recelebrate it.

In celebrating the eucharistic sacrifice, we are introduced each time into the mystery of God himself and also into the entire profundity of the human reality. The Eucharist is the announcement of death and resurrection. The paschal mystery is expressed therein as the beginning of a new time and as the final expectation.

A Fundamental Choice: That of Humanity

In the pursuit of the well-being of peoples and nations, we must continually make choices. There are new choices to make on the basis of political principles and priorities, on the basis of economic laws or in the light of practical necessities. But there is one choice that should always be made, whatever the context of the problem may be, and it is the fundamental choice: the choice for or against humanity.

No matter what responsibility or authority a person may have, no one can avoid this choice.

Shall we work for the good of humanity or against it? Shall the total good of the human person be the ultimate criterion of our actions and our programs?

The State Is a Service for the People

The state, which has the sovereignty of society as its justification and is entrusted with the defense of independence, must never lose sight of its principal objective—the common good of all its citizens, without any distinction whatever, and not simply the well-being of a particular group or category.

The state must reject everything that is not worthy of the freedom and the human rights of its people, putting aside every element such as the abuse of authority, corruption, domination over the weak, denying the people the right to participate in political life and decisions, and the tyranny and use of violence and terrorism.

Here again I do not hesitate to refer to the truth about man. Without the acceptance of the truth about man, his dignity, and his eternal destiny, there cannot exist among nations that fundamental trust which is one of the root elements of every human undertaking. Neither can public office be seen as what it really is: a service for the people that finds its sole justification in concern for the good of all.

OCTOBER 17

Fewer Slogans and More Truths

Nations have the duty to review their positions without ceasing so as to become involved in a movement that passes from a less human situation to a more human one in national as well as international life.

This demands the capacity to renounce slogans and stereotyped positions in order to seek and affirm truth, which is the force of peace. This also signifies the readiness to set the ideal and the dignity of the human person at the basis or in the heart of every political, social, or economic concern.

The harm of non-truth is manifested in acute fashion in the present world with the threats of war that persist or manifest themselves anew. But this harm is also visible in other areas, such as those of justice, development, and the rights of man.

Modern man seems to be threatened by his own creations and runs the risk of losing the true meaning of reality and the true meaning of things, alienating himself in his own deductions, because he does not constantly relate all things to a central vision concerning the dignity, inviolability, and sacred character of human life and of every human being.

Harmony Among Peoples Transcends Prejudices and Rivalries

Every nation makes its cultural contribution to the family of nations, and by means of the legitimate expression of values and traditions it becomes possible to create a harmony among peoples that transcends partisan differences, prejudices, and rivalries.

Such harmony—built on respect and openness in contacts with the values of others, and in a particular way moral and spiritual values—contributes to making possible a concerted action to deal with problems that go beyond the boundaries of single nations.

Disincarnated Political Activity Becomes Alienation

Invoking the respect for moral and spiritual values in the sphere of international collaboration, I touch upon a theme that I believe is basic to all of the relations that exist in society.

All of the structures that are created to express needs and aspirations are concerned with the human person, because they ultimately serve every human person and the human community as a whole.

This holds good in a particular way for what concerns political structures and activities. In my address before the General Assembly of the United Nations, I said that all political activity "comes from man, is exercised by man, and is for man. And if political activity is cut off from this fundamental relationship and finality, if it becomes in a way its own end, it loses much of its reason to exist.

"Even more, it can also give rise to a specific alienation; it can become extraneous to man; it can come to contradict humanity itself. In reality, what justifies the existence of any political activity is the service to man, concerned and responsible attention to the essential problems and duties of his earthly existence in its social dimension and significance on which also the good of each person depends."

OCTOBER 20

Violence—a Crime Against Humanity

Peace cannot be established by violence; peace can never flourish in a climate of terror, intimidation, and death.

Violence is unacceptable as a solution to problems, [it] is unworthy of man.

Violence is a lie, for it goes against the truth of our faith, the truth of our humanity.

Violence destroys what it claims to defend: the dignity, the life, the freedom of human beings.

Violence is a crime against humanity.

OCTOBER 21

The Laity: Citizens of Earth and of Heaven

The role of the laity in the mission of the Church goes in two directions. In union with your pastors and aided by their guidance, you build up the communion of the faithful. In addition, as responsible citizens, you permeate the society in which you live with the leaven of the Gospel, acting on its economic, social, political, cultural, and intellectual dimensions.

When you faithfully carry out these two roles as citizens of both the earthly city and the kingdom of heaven, you are fulfilling the words of Christ: "You are the salt of the earth. . . . You are the light of the world" (Mt 5:13–14).

As lay people, you are called to take an active part in the sacramental and liturgical life of the Church, and in a special way in the eucharistic sacrifice. At the same time, you are called to energetically spread the Gospel by works of charity and by your diligent commitment in accord with the gifts that each of you has received.

In every Christian community, whether it is the "domestic Church" constituted by the family, or the parish that collaborates with the priest, or the diocese united around the bishop, lay people strive as did the followers of Christ in the first century to remain faithful to the teaching of the apostles, faithful to fraternal service, faithful to prayer and the celebration of the Eucharist (cf. Acts 2:42).

OCTOBER 22

We Can Rely on Christ Now and Forever

Christ is with us: this certitude fills our hearts with an immense peace and a profound joy. We know we can rely on him here, above all now and forever. He is the friend who understands us and sustains us in dark moments, because he is the "man of sorrows who is well acquainted with suffering" (Is 53:3). He is the companion along the way who restores warmth to our hearts, enlightening them about the treasures of wisdom contained in the Scriptures (cf. Lk 24:32).

He is the living bread come down from heaven who can enkindle in our mortal flesh the spark of life that does not die (cf. Jn 6:51).

Cultivating a Hunger for the Word of God

We must begin our bearing witness to the truth by cultivating a hunger for the Word of God and a desire to receive and to have in our heart the life-giving message of the Gospel in all its fullness.

When you attentively heed the voice of the Savior and then put it into practice, you truly participate in the mission of the Church at the service of truth. You bear witness before the world to your firm faith in the promise made by God through Isaiah: "As the rain and the snow come down from heaven and do not return to it without watering the earth and making it bud and flourish, so that it yields seed for the sower and bread to be eaten, so will it be with the word that goes forth from my mouth: it will not return empty to me, without working what I desire and without accomplishing the purpose for which I sent it forth" (Is 55:10–11). You can be messengers of truth only if you are first of all hearers of the Word of God.

Through the Medium of Culture Man Creates Himself

My origin, my formation, and my history have taught me to place a very great value on the power that culture exercises over every people. During the trip to my Poland, I expressed this conviction in these words: "Culture is an expression of man, a confirmation of humanity. Man creates culture and by means of culture he creates himself. He creates himself by virtue of the inner force of his spirit, thought, will, and heart.

"At the same time, he creates culture in communion with others. Culture is an expression of communion of thought and shared collaboration on the part of human beings. It is born to the service of the common good and it becomes an essential good of the human community."

The Prayer of Christ Is the Reason for Our Hope

Because we believe in Christ and in the "unfathomable riches of Christ" (Eph 3:8), we feel ourselves guided by the Spirit in removing the divisions in faith that impair our common witness to the Lord and his kingdom. This will enable us to better serve our neighbor and to bring with greater efficacy the good news of salvation to the world which continues to see in us a divided Christ.

In any case, we know that Christ prayed for unity, and that the Father listens to his prayer. The prayer of Christ is the reason for our hope, and we know that "hope does not disappoint us" (Rom 5:5).

Living in Unity and Strengthening Unity

My counsel is: live in unity and strengthen this unity. Therefore, put aside every division.

Membership in the same body of Christ does not tolerate exclusion, contempt, or hatred. It is a summons to collaboration, peace, and the fraternity of love.

Be workers of peace.

A Vocation—the Fruit of Faith

Vocation derives from a faith that is living and coherent even to extreme consequences, which opens up for man the final perspective, that is, the perspective of the encounter with God himself, who is alone worthy of a love "above everything," an exclusive and conjugal love. This love consists in the giving of our entire human person, body and soul, to the one who gave himself completely to us men.

This vocation, once accepted, once solemnly confirmed by means of vows, must be continually nourished by the riches of faith, not only when it brings inner joy with it, but also when it is connected with difficulties, aridity, and inner suffering, known as "the night of the soul."

This vocation is a special treasure of the Church, which can never cease to pray that the spirit of Jesus Christ may stir up religious vocations in souls.

The Missionary Experience in the Church

The living testimonial of the maturity of every Church is not only its openness to the Word of God, to the salvific good, but also the capacity of giving to others what she herself is living. With this giving, she not only manifests her maturity but also deepens and solidifies it. Therefore, like the whole Church, even local churches desire to become missionary, to become the subject of this "missionary aspect" of the Church.

Think Well to Act Well

In right thinking there is the presupposition of right acting; and right acting holds the hope of a durable solution for the serious ills that afflict mankind.

The Human Spirit Is Above Nature

Man's difference from nature is greater than his likeness to it. This is a bold statement, and it takes faith to accept it. In any case, reason that is devoid of prejudices is not opposed to such a truth about man. On the contrary, it sees therein a complement to what emerges from the analysis of the human reality and above all from the human spirit.

Matrimony: the Boldest Contract There Is

Christian spouses have promised one another to place in common all that they are and all that they have. This is the boldest contract there is, and at the same time the most wonderful!

The union of their bodies! Willed by God himself as the expression of the most profound communion of their spirit and their heart, and accomplished with both respect and tenderness, it renews the dynamism and the freshness of their solemn pledge, of their first "Yes."

The union of their characters! To love a person is to love what he is, to love him to the point of cultivating in oneself the antidote for his weaknesses and his failings—for example, practicing tranquillity and patience if the beloved is notoriously lacking in them.

The union of hearts! The shadings that differentiate the love of man from the love of woman are innumerable. A very unifying common aspect is that of the joys—and even prior to it, of the sufferings—of the heart.

But it is above all in the common love for the children that the union of hearts is strengthened.

† † †

November

After the Condemnation of Death Lies the Future Life

Man who in accord with the laws of nature is "condemned to death," man who lives with the prospect of his body's destruction, this man exists at the same time with the prospect of the future life and is called to glory.

The solemnity of All Saints places before the eyes of our faith all those who have already reached the fullness of their call to union with God. The day that commemorates the dead focuses our thoughts on those who, having left this world, are waiting in expiation to reach that fullness of love which union with God requires.

The Peace and Light of the Dead, Hope of the Earth

"You are dust and into dust you shall return" (Gn 3:19). All the cemeteries of the world constitute an unceasing confirmation of these words—whether they are the places where our popes, bishops, and priests are laid or those in which we pray for our dear ones: parents, brothers, sisters, friends, and benefactors.

There are cemeteries that contain the great and honored ones of every nation and those that house the simple, at times possibly unknown and forgotten, who no longer have anyone to light a candle on their grave on the day of the dead. In all these sites of the earth, far and near, there rises the same prayer for peace and light.

This peace and eternal light constitute the hope of those still living on earth. This peace and light constitute the expression of the life possessed by those who are enveloped in the death of the body.

Remembering the Dead— Remembering the Newborn

In human life, dying is connected with being born and being born with dying, in the very way that the old year is connected with the new.

If, therefore, we remember the dead, we must also remember those who have seen the light of life, who have come into the world, who have been born.

With this thought, we embrace all of the families in which a man is born, just as one day in the stable of Bethlehem the Son of God made Man was born. And by being born there he has imprinted a seal on the birth of all men: "He has indeed given men the power to become children of God."

Man Cannot Be Made a Slave to Anyone or to Anything

Man cannot abdicate from himself, nor from the place to which he belongs in the visible world. Man cannot become a slave to things, to material riches, to consumerism, to economic systems or to that which he himself produces. Man cannot be made a slave to anyone or to anything.

Man cannot eliminate the transcendental—in the last analysis, God—without cutting himself off from his total being. Man in the end will only be able to find light for his own "mystery" in the mystery of Christ.

The True Christian
Is the Eucharistic Soul

Without Christ it is fatal to get lost, become confused, and indeed to lapse into despair! This was intuited by Dante Alighieri, man of the world and of faith, poetic genius and skilled theologian. In his paraphrase of the Our Father, recited by the souls being purified, he teaches that in the harsh desert of life, without intimate union with Christ— "the manna" of the New Testament and "the bread come down from heaven"—the person who wants to go forward solely through his own forces in reality goes backward: "Give us this day the daily manna / without which in this harsh desert / the person who races to get ahead goes backward" (Purgatory, XI, 13–15).

The Eucharist alone makes it possible to live the heroic virtues of Christianity: charity unto the forgiveness of enemies, love for those who make us suffer, and giving one's life for one's neighbor; chastity in every age and situation of life; and especially in suffering and when one is shaken by the silence of God in the dramas of history or of one's own existence.

Therefore, be ever eucharistic souls, so as to be true Christians.

Work—God's Summons
to Build a New World

Work must not be a mere necessity but it is to be regarded as a true vocation, a summons from God to build a new world in which justice and brotherhood live together, as an anticipation of the kingdom of God where there will certainly be neither lack nor limitation.

Work must be the means whereby all creation is subjected to the dignity of the human being and the child of God. Work offers the opportunity of committing oneself together with the entire community without resentments, without bitterness, and without hatred, but with the universal love of Christ that excludes no one and embraces all.

We Cannot Decapitate Man

It is beautiful to note how the Christian religion proclaims the primacy of God over all things and how it thereby gives rise—in temporal realities—to the primacy of man.

It is beautiful to observe how this primacy constitutes the motivation that stimulates and justifies that social dynamism and that civil progress on which the industrial phenomenon impresses its inevitable motion.

And it is precisely in virtue of the recognition of this primacy that nowadays we are emerging from the primitive stage of the industrial era, when it was thought that social harmony resulted solely from the determinism of the economic conditions at play. On the contrary, it is now known to all how many misfortunes are caused by the quest for the human well-being founded exclusively and uniquely on economic goods and on a materialistic approach to life, which does not serve but rather enslaves man.

It must not be forgotten, in this respect, that work is for man and not man for work. If such were not the case, man would return to being a slave.

Now if man is the prime value, we cannot diminish him nor decapitate him, denying to him his essential projection toward transcendence, that is, toward God, who has made man his collaborator.

In this superior vision, work—the pain and at the same time the reward of human activity—comprises another contribution, that is, the essentially religious one, which has been felicitously expressed by the Benedictine motto: *ora et labora* [work and pray]!

The religious fact confers on human work an animating and redeeming spirituality. Such a connection between work and religion reflects the mysterious but real alliance that exists between human action and God's providential action.

NOVEMBER 8

Only Love Can Avoid the Tragedy of Cain

Christianity does not command us to close our eyes to difficult human problems. It does not permit us to neglect and refuse to see unjust social or international situations.

What Christianity does forbid is to seek solutions to these situations by the ways of hatred, by the murdering of defenseless people, by the methods of terrorism.

Christianity understands and recognizes the noble and just struggle for justice; but Christianity is decisively opposed to fomenting hatred and to promoting or provoking violence or struggle for the sake of "struggle."

The commandment "You shall not kill" must be binding on the conscience of humanity if the terrible tragedy and destiny of Cain is not to be repeated.

The Hand Extended
Toward the Disinherited

If the Church takes part in the defense or the advancement of man's dignity, she does so in conformity with her mission, which, even though it is religious in character rather than social or political, cannot do less than consider man in his whole being.

The Lord has set down in the parable of the good Samaritan the model of the person concerned with all human necessities (Lk 10:29ff), and has declared that he will identify himself with the disinherited, the infirm, the imprisoned, the hungry, and the abandoned to whom a hand is extended (Mt 25:31ff).

The Church has understood from this and other pages of the Gospel (Mk 6:33–44) that her evangelical mission has as an indispensable part the commitment to justice and the work for man's advancement (cf. final Document of the Synod of bishops, October 1971) and that between evangelization and human advancement there are very strong ties of the anthropological, theological, and charitable order (EN, no. 31); so that "evangelization would not be complete unless one took account of the reciprocal connection that in the course of time is established between the Gospel and the concrete, personal, and social life of man" (EN, no. 29).

On the other hand, we must keep in mind that the action of the Church in areas such as those of human advancement, development, justice, and the rights of the person is always intended to be at the service of man, as she sees him in the Christian vision of her anthropology.

Indeed, the Church does not need to have recourse to ideological systems in order to love, defend, and collaborate in the liberation of man. It is at the center of the message of which she is the depositary and the proclaimer that she finds inspiration to work on behalf of brotherhood, justice, and peace in opposition to all domination, slavery, discrimination, violence, attempts on religious freedom, aggressions against man, and with great attentiveness to life (GS, nos. 26, 27 and 29).

NOVEMBER 10

Freedom and Reconciliation

The Church has the duty to announce the liberation of millions of human beings, the duty to help so that this liberation is solidified (EN, no 30). However, she also has the corresponding duty of proclaiming this liberation in its integral and profound meaning as Jesus has announced and effected it (EN, no. 31).

"Liberation from all that oppresses man, which above all constitutes salvation from sin and from the evil one, in the joy of knowing God and being known by him" (EN, no. 39).

Liberation made up of reconciliation and pardon.

Liberation that erupts from the reality of being children of God, who can call out "Abba, Father" (Rom 8:15), by virtue of which we recognize in every man a brother whose heart can be transformed by God's mercy.

Liberation that directs us by the force of charity to communion, whose summit and fullness we find in the Lord.

Liberation as the overcoming of the diverse slaveries and idols that man fashions for himself, and as the growth of the new man.

To Proclaim the Gospel
Is to Encounter the Voice of the Holy Spirit

To proclaim the Gospel, to teach, means to encounter the living person with human thought who continually—and always in a different way and in new areas—seeks the truth. He questions and looks for the answer.

To find the authentic answer that conforms to reality and is both exact and persuasive, he undertakes researches that are at times difficult and thankless. The thirst for truth is one of the undeniable expressions of the human spirit.

To proclaim the Gospel, to teach, signifies a meeting of this voice of the human spirit on various levels, but above all on the highest level, where the quest for truth is carried out in a methodical manner, in specialized institutes that serve for research and the transmission of the results and inquiries, that is, for the transmission of teaching.

The Church Is Not Tied
to Any Political System

By virtue of her proper mission and nature, the Church is not tied to any definite form of culture, nor to any political, economic, or social system.

Precisely because of this universality of hers, she can enter into communion with different cultures and realities, culminating in mutual enrichment.

By virtue of this same universality, she is also capable of creating a very close tie between different human communities and between nations, on condition that these acknowledge and respect her right to freedom in carrying out her specific mission.

The Terrible Threat
of Nuclear Arms

Our contemporary world is witnessing the growth of the terrible threat of the destruction of some by others, especially with the proliferation of nuclear arms. The positioning of these arms and the climate of threat that they provoke have brought it about that millions of persons and entire peoples are already experiencing the reduction of their possibilities for peace and freedom.

Under these conditions, the great society of workers precisely in the name of the moral force found therein must ask categorically and clearly: Where, in what atmosphere, and why have the confines of the noble struggle for justice, the struggle for the good of man and in particular the most marginal and needy man, been breached?

Where, in what atmosphere, and why has this moral and creative force been transformed into a destructive force, into hatred, and into the new forms of collective egotism that raise the specter of the threat of a possibility of a struggle on the part of all against all and of a monstrous self-destruction?

Our age demands that we ask ourselves this question—which is such a fundamental one. It is a categorical imperative of consciences: of every man, of entire societies, and in particular of those burdened with the principal responsibility for today and for the future of the world. In such a question is manifested the moral force represented by the worker, by the world of work, and at the same time by all men.

Joy Is the Keynote
of the Christian Message

Christ came to bring joy: joy to children, joy to parents, joy to families and to friends, joy to workers and to scholars, joy to the sick and to the elderly, joy to all humanity. In a true sense, joy is the keynote of the Christian message. . . .

We are an Easter people and "Alleluia" is our song. With St. Paul I exhort you: "Rejoice in the Lord always, I say it again, rejoice" (Phil 4:4).

Rejoice because Jesus has come into the world!
Rejoice because Jesus has died upon the cross!
Rejoice because he rose from the dead!
Rejoice because in baptism he washed away our sins!
Rejoice because Jesus has come to set us free!
And rejoice because he is the Master of our life!

The Vigil That Makes Us a Church

There is a night in which by keeping vigil at your
    sepulcher we are more than ever Church—
it is the night in which desperation and hope struggle
    within us:
this struggle always surpasses all the struggles of
    history entirely pervading them.
(Do they lose their meaning, or only then do they
    acquire it?)
In this night the rite of the earth is reunited with its
    beginning,

a thousand years as one single night: Night of vigil at
your sepulcher.

Love for One Another
Must Be the Hallmark of Your Lives

A city needs a soul if it is to become a true home for
human beings. You the people must give it this soul. And
how do you do this? By loving one another. Love for one
another must be the hallmark of your lives.

In the Gospel Jesus Christ tells us: "You shall love your
neighbor as yourself" (Mt 22:29). This commandment must
be your inspiration in forming true human relationships
among yourselves, so that nobody will ever feel alone or
unwanted, or much less, rejected, despised, or hated.

Jesus himself will give you the power of fraternal love.
And every neighborhood, every block, every street will become a true community because you will want it so, and Jesus will help you to bring it about.

To Pass through Death
Is Part of Easter

At the right time hope rises from all the places
subject to death—
hope is its counterpart,
wherein the world that dies reveals life anew.
In the streets the passersby with the short jackets and
    hair falling to the shoulders
cut with the blade of their step

the space of the great mystery
which in each of them is extended between death
    and hope:
a space that radiates toward the heights like the stone
    of solar light
overturned at the entrance to the sepulcher.

In this space, the most perfect measure of the world,
you are present,
and therefore I have a meaning, and to slip into the
    tomb,
to pass away in death,
to be dissolved in the dust of unrepeatable atoms—
is for me a part of your Easter.

To Make Use of Creation
Is to Render Glory to God

From the very beginning, God has entrusted man with the nature that he has created. To make use of creation for an integral and solidary human advancement, which enables man to attain his full spiritual dimension, is to render glory to God.

Man must therefore strive to respect creation and discover its laws so that the service to man will be assured. Great progress has been made in the field of ecology and great effort has been expended, but much still remains to be done to educate people to respect nature, to preserve it and better it, and also to reduce or prevent the consequences of so-called natural catastrophes.

The Vicious Circle of Poverty
and Underdevelopment

It is common knowledge that the abyss between the excessively rich minority and the very poor majority is a most grave symptom in the life of every society. The same must be said, with even stronger insistence, about the abyss that divides individual countries as well as regions of the earth.

The fact that such glaring disparities can exist constitutes a great contradiction of our day and of our age; the same can be said about the gulf that separates the poor countries from the rich, and that is becoming even greater instead of diminishing, at the very time when peoples have become more aware of their interdependence than ever before.

Isn't it sad to ascertain that the energies—so laudable in themselves—of international organizations and the various nations, concretized in bilateral or multilateral initiatives, have been unable to draw the poorest countries out of the vicious circle of poverty and underdevelopment?

Why have these energies failed to achieve better and more durable results? Because they have not given hope to developing countries: the hope that their own resources, fraternal assistance, and especially the hard labor of their citizens would have rendered them capable of charting their own development and satisfying their essential needs.

The Importance of Revitalizing
the North-South Dialogue

I am convinced that we are all in accord concerning the fact that the only way to eliminate inequalities is by the coordinated cooperation of all countries in the spirit of true association. In this context, much has been said and written about the importance of revitalizing what has been defined as the North-South dialogue.

Without subscribing to an overly simplistic view of the world divided into a rich North and a poor South, we must concede that this distinction has a certain basis in fact, since the Northern countries generally control the economy and industry of the world.

The Holy See cannot fail to encourage every initiative put forth to take such a situation honestly into consideration and to reach an understanding among all parties regarding the necessary action to be undertaken.

The difficulties and points of controversy that divide the richest from the poorest nations cannot be dealt with so long as a prejudicial attitude exists. These subjects must be faced in a spirit of honest evaluation of reality and with a generous willingness to share.

NOVEMBER 21

Dialogue Is Not
"The Art of Confusing Essential Concepts"

We must be particularly disposed to dialogue. But we must first define its principal meaning and its basic conditions.

According to the thought of Paul VI, and we can say also of the Council, "dialogue" certainly signifies openness and the capacity to understand another person to his very roots: his history, the path he has followed, and the inspirations that animate him.

It in no way signifies either indifferentism or the "art of confusing essential concepts," although this art is too often regarded as the equivalent of the attitude to "dialogue."

And much less does it signify "to veil" the truths of one's personal creed.

The Prophetic Charisma
and the Ecclesiastical Magisterium

In an age when there is so much talk about the "prophetic charisma"—not always using this concept in its exact meaning—we must profoundly renew and reconstruct the awareness of the prophetic charisma linked with the episcopal ministry of the teachers of the faith and the "leaders of the flock" who, according to an apt analogy, incarnate in their lives the words of Christ about the "good shepherd."

The good shepherd is concerned with the pasturing and feeding of his sheep. And here I am thinking particularly of the theological publications that are speedily diffused within a wide radius in many circles and whose essential ideas are popularized in magazines. In accord with their qualities, their profundity, and their sense of the Church, these either teach and deepen the [people's] faith or on the contrary disturb that faith and cause it to dissolve.

Freedom at All Levels
of Political and Social Life

I know what it means to vindicate the right of self-determination, in the name of justice and national dignity. But this is only a stage, because it is still necessary for self-determination to remain effective and to be accompanied by a real participation by the citizenry working out their destiny: in this way even progress can be more equally beneficial to all.

Hence, freedom must act on all levels of political and social life. The unity of a people requires also an action that is persevering, respectful of legitimate differences, and at the same time carried out in a harmonious manner. But nowadays so many hopes are permitted and so many possibilities are offered that an immense joy fills my heart corresponding to the trust that I place in men of good will, who desire the common good.

NOVEMBER 24

The Free Man
Is the Man Who Is Totally Consecrated

The supreme freedom is the freedom that results from the complete offering of self to God. The free man is the man who is totally consecrated to God—one might say: to the service of God! This is the man totally consecrated to service—like Christ, the servant of Yahweh of the Old Testament, consecrated to service even unto death, and like Mary, the servant of the Lord.

The man most free is the man totally consecrated. This is the greatest program. In this area of the greatest program everyone discovers the gift, because everyone has his own gift, the gift of God that he must render fruitful all his life.

This gift is possessed by the man of letters and the man of science, the miner and the metal worker. The gift of God is possessed by the engineer and the student and the child—it is possessed by all and no one is excluded. This gift is the call to overcome evil with good.

The Responsibility
to Bear Witness to the Truth

All of the faithful have a task to carry out in the mission of the Church in confrontations with truth. That is why in "Redemptor hominis" [The Redeemer of Man] I stated: "The Church's responsibility for divine truth must be increasingly shared by all in various ways—the specialists in the various disciplines, those who represent the natural sciences and letters, doctors, jurists, artists and technicians, teachers at various levels and with different specializations. As members of the People of God, they all have their own part to play in Christ's prophetic mission and service of divine truth" (no. 19).

In the communion of the faithful and especially in the heart of the local Christian community, special attention must be given to this responsibility to bear witness to the truth.

The Study of Scripture
Is Prayer

Jesus was able to complete his mission thanks to his total union with the Father, because he was one with him: in his condition of pilgrim along the paths of our earth (*viator*—wayfarer), he was already in possession of the end (*comprehensor*—possessor) toward which he was to lead others.

To be able to continue Christ's mission effectively, the priest must himself in some way already have reached the goal to which he wishes to lead others. He can reach it by assiduous contemplation of the mystery of God, nourished by the study of Scripture, a study that becomes transformed into prayer.

Fidelity to the moments and modes of personal prayer, the most official prayer of the "Hours," and also the worthy and generous fulfillment of the sacred acts of the ministry all contribute to sanctify the priest and lead him to an experience of the mysterious and fascinating presence of the living God, enabling him to act with power in the human atmosphere all around him.

Faith Is Not a Pretty Garment for the Time of Childhood

Stop thinking to yourselves or saying aloud that the Christian faith is good solely for children and simple folk. If the faith still appears to be such, it is because adolescents and adults have seriously neglected to make their faith grow in accord with the rhythm of their human development.

Faith is not a pretty garment for the time of childhood. Faith is a gift of God, a current of light and strength that comes from him and that must illumine and vitalize all sectors of life, as it gradually becomes rooted in responsibility.

The Paradox of Suffering

Be prepared to encounter at times opposition, scorn, and derision. True disciples are not greater than their master. Their crosses are like the passion and cross of Christ:

mysterious source of fruitfulness. This paradox of suffering that is offered up and becomes fruitful is verified over the course of twenty centuries in the history of the Church.

Conversion of Heart and Sanctity of Life for Reunion in Christ

We must thank the Lord that the oppositions of former times have yielded to an effort toward union based on mutual esteem, search for truth, and charity. Nevertheless, we know that the magnificent goal we seek, in obedience to the Lord, has not yet been attained.

In order to attain it there is need—with God's grace—for "the conversion of heart and the sanctity of life," which as the Second Vatican Council has stressed constitute, together with prayer for unity, "the soul of the ecumenical movement."

Every initiative geared toward unity would be vain if it were deprived of this foundation, if it were not based on the constant and at times arduous quest for complete truth and sanctity. This quest brings us closer to Christ and, through him, brings us really closer to one another.

Is Progress the Knowledge of Objects and Things?

Do the contemporary development and progress in which we participate constitute the fruit of the alliance with the divine wisdom? Aren't they merely an ever more exact knowledge of objects and things on which is constructed the dizzying progress of technology? Doesn't man who is the architect of this progress become ever more the object of that progress?

Thus, that alliance with wisdom is being ever more destroyed around him—the eternal alliance with wisdom which is the source of culture, that is to say, of man's true growth.

† † †

December

The Man Who Does Not Understand the Need to Be Converted Is an Unhappy Man

Be converted! We place ourselves before God—each and every one of us—with this cry that was uttered two thousand years ago by the psalmist, who was at once king and sinner.

"Have mercy on me, O God, according to your mercy; in your great goodness blot out my sin. . . ."

So many generations have gone by, yet these words have lost none of their authenticity and power. The man who strives to live in the truth accepts them as his own. He utters them as if they were his own.

The man who is incapable of identifying himself with the truth of these words is an unhappy man. If he does not examine his conscience in the light of these words, they will judge him alone—without him.

Closer to God During Advent

Advent leads each of us, so to speak, "into the inner chamber of our heart" to live therein the closeness of God, responding to the question that the human heart must put to itself in the whole of its inner truth.

And when we sincerely and honestly put this question

to ourselves, in the sight of God, we always fulfill what John spoke about at the Jordan in his fascinating metaphor: here is the winnowing fan to clear out the threshing floor anew. It enables the farmer to gather the wheat in the barn and makes the chaff burn with unquenchable fire (Lk 3:17).

This is the very thing that must be done more than once. We must focus on ourselves, with the aid of that light which the Holy Spirit will not deny us, and delineate and separate the good and the evil in us. We must call each by name and not deceive ourselves. Then this will be a true "baptism," which will renew our souls. The one who "is near" (Phil 4:5) comes to baptize us in the Holy Spirit and in fire (Lk 3:18).

Advent—the preparation for the great solemnity of the Incarnation—must be connected with such a purification.

Progress Is a New Birth

In the Gospel there is an invitation to progress. Today the whole world is full of invitations to progress. No one wants to be a "non-progressivist."

It is a question of knowing in what way we can and must "be progressivist," and in what true progress consists. We cannot pass tranquilly over these questions.

Advent bears within itself the deepest meaning of progress.

Advent reminds us every year that human life cannot be a state of stagnation. It must be a progress.

Advent shows us in what this progress consists.

The Measure of Man Is God

The measure of things and events of the created world is man, but the measure of man is God. Therefore, man must always return to this source, to this unique measure, who is God incarnate in Jesus Christ, if he wants to be man and if the world is to be human.

Church-Mother and Church-Bride

The Church of Jesus Christ and the apostles is at the same time Church-Mother and Church-Bride. These biblical expressions reveal in a clear manner how profoundly the mission of woman is inscribed in the mystery of the Church.

We could together discover the multiform significance of this mission—going hand in hand with the feminine world of today—basing ourselves on the riches which from the beginning the Creator has placed in the heart of woman!

The Entire Church Is Involved in the Responsibility for the Gospel

Not only is the Church grateful for what has been accomplished by catechists in the past, but she is also confident for the future. In spite of new circumstances, new exigencies, and new obstacles, the importance of this grand apostolate has not been diminished, because it will always be necessary to develop an initial faith, and to guide the people to the fullness of the Christian life.

A growing awareness of the dignity and importance of the task of the catechist is a consequence of the Second Vatican Council's insistence on the fact that the entire Church is involved in responsibility for the Gospel.

Only with the collaboration of her catechists will the Church be able to adequately respond to the challenge I described in my apostolic exhortation on catechesis in our time: "As the twentieth century draws to a close, the Church is bidden by God and by events—each of them a call from him—to renew her trust in catechetical activity as a prime aspect of her mission.

"She is bidden to offer catechesis her best resources in people and energy, without sparing effort, toil, or material means, in order to organize it better and to train qualified personnel. This is no mere human calculation; it is an attitude of faith."

DECEMBER 7

United to Renew the World

The present youthful generation, even when it avails itself of the comforts offered by a consumer civilization, cautions that so much prodigality conceals an illusory seductiveness, and that we cannot stop at the jovial experience of materialistic opulence.

You young people are pursuing a continual quest—to live it is already to correspond to the Christian vocation—the true value of life and your personal responsibility.

In such a quest we cannot proceed in isolation, precisely because of the fragility of the individual exposed to the most diverse attacks.

The vitality of that social renewal to which all of you

aspire can be established and preserved by the adherence to a group, the spontaneity and homogeneity of a circle of friends, the constructive discussion of ideas and initiatives, and mutual sustenance.

Mary and Youth

I wish to bring the youth of the whole world and the entire Church close to Mary, who is the mother of the true love.

She bears in herself an indestructible sign of never-fading youth and beauty. I desire and I pray that young people may come close to her, have confidence in her, and entrust to her the life that lies before each of them; may they love her with a simple and ardent love of their heart.

She alone is able to respond to that love in the best way.

We Must Be Mature Personalities

Ideological confusion gives birth to psychologically immature and flawed personalities. Precisely because of this reason the modern world is involved in a laborious quest for models, and most of the time remains deluded, defeated, and humiliated.

Therefore, we must be mature personalities, who know how to control our own emotions, assuming our proper roles of responsibility and leadership, who seek to fulfill ourselves in the place and in the work in which we find ourselves.

Our time demands serenity and courage to accept reality as it is, without depressing criticisms and without utopias, in order to love and save it.

The Eucharist Is the Most Intimate and Transforming Encounter with Christ

Every encounter with Christ leaves deep marks. It may be a nocturnal encounter, like that of Nicodemus; it may be a casual encounter, like that of the Samaritan woman; it may be a sought-out encounter, like that of the penitent woman; it may be a supplicatory encounter, like that of the blind man at the gates of Jericho; or it may be a curiosity encounter, like that of Zacchaeus; or again it may be an intimate encounter, like the encounter of each of the apostles when called to follow Christ; or an overpowering encounter, like that of Paul on the road to Damascus.

However, the most intimate and transforming encounter is the one that takes place at the table of the eucharistic mystery, that is, at the table of the bread of the Lord.

In the Knowledge of Christ You Have a Key to the Understanding of the Needs of the World

"Let the message of Christ, in all its richness, find a home with you" (Col 3:16). In the knowledge of Christ you have the key to the Gospel. In the knowledge of Christ you have an understanding of the needs of the world. Since he became one with us in all things but sin, your union with Jesus of Nazareth could never, and will never, be an obstacle to understanding and responding to the needs of the world.

And finally, in the knowledge of Christ, you will not only discover and come to understand the limitations of human wisdom and of human solutions to the needs of humanity, but you will also experience the power of Jesus, and the value of human reason and human endeavor when they are taken up in the strength of Jesus, when they are redeemed in Christ.

By the Action of the Holy Spirit the Church Is Built Up Day After Day

Divine law is the sole standard of human liberty and is given to us in the Gospel of Christ, the Gospel of Redemption. But fidelity to the Gospel of Redemption will never be possible without the action of the Holy Spirit, who guards the life-giving message entrusted to the Church.

It is the Holy Spirit who ensures the faithful transmission of the Gospel into the lives of all of us. It is by the action of the Holy Spirit that the Church is built up day after day into a kingdom: a kingdom of truth and life, a kingdom of holiness and grace, a universal kingdom of justice, love, and peace.

A Palpitation for the Heart of Man

Advent is the history of the initial relationships between God and man. As soon as the Christian becomes aware of his supernatural vocation, he welcomes the mys-

tery of God's coming to his own soul, and his heart instant-
ly palpitates and pulsates with this reality, since it is none
other than the very life of Christianity.

The Universal Solidarity of Bethlehem

The stable of Bethlehem is the primary place of man's
solidarity: the solidarity of one man with another and of all
men with all, and chiefly with those for whom "there is no
room in the inn" (Lk 2:7), and whose rights are not recognized.

The Temptation That Says: "Sin Does Not Exist"

Innumerable are the temptations that assail men and
that lead to sin. In the contemporary world, they are truly
many. Among them, the most dangerous temptation is the
one that says: "Sin does not exist," the one that does not
want to regard sin as sin.

Thus, for example—it is even frightening to say it—
people at times seek to persuade a woman bearing a conceived baby beneath her heart to commit a crime of homi-
cide by saying: "It is only a simple intervention. . . ."

People give this kind of description to this horrible
temptation not only to commit a sin but a crime as well.
They seek to deaden the vigilance of human and Christian
consciences. They want to blot sin out of man's conscience.
And this is a particular temptation; we might say: a satanic
temptation.

When we read, in a particular way in Genesis, the description of man's first sin and first temptation, we see that

it consisted precisely in deadening vigilance. It consisted in the fact that sin was not called sin. In fact, the tempter said: "You will be like gods. . . ." Isn't this what is being repeated to contemporary man?

The temptation that in a particular way weighs down on our age is called atheism. Man is told: God does not exist! The first human beings were told: "You will be like gods!" Contemporary man is told: God does not exist! And everything is done, entire systems and entire programs are created, to separate man from God—to uproot God from his mind and his heart, to extirpate God.

DECEMBER 16

Truth—a Right of Man

Those who follow the light of divine revelation, those who believe in Jesus Christ, serve truth in a particular way, rest in truth, and offer their lives for truth.

It is necessary to speak about all of this also because the desire for truth, or simply truth itself, is a right of man—a basic right that shapes his life.

Respect for this right determines the form of human life—individual, personal, and even social life.

DECEMBER 17

God Has Clothed Himself with Time so that Man Might Clothe Himself with Eternity

God, in becoming man on Christmas eve, willed to clothe himself with time; just as every man and every creature are subjected to human time, so he too subjected himself to it.

He entered into our human time and has made this human time of ours a definitive time of salvation.

When God was made man, all of us were grasped by the time of salvation. Thus, the history of man, the history of peoples and nations, the history of epochs, races, and cultures, the history of all humanity becomes the history of salvation.

Christmas Is a Ray of Light for All

In spite of the pain that at times enters our life, Christmas is a ray of light for all, because it reveals to us the love of God and makes us feel the presence of Jesus with all, especially with those who suffer. Precisely for this reason Jesus willed to be born in the poverty and abandonment of a stable and to be placed in a manger.

In Confession There Is Mercy Not Condemnation

The confessionals of the world, in which men lay bare their sins, do not speak of God's severity but rather of his merciful goodness. And as many as approach the confessional—sometimes after years and burdened with grave sins—find the desired relief upon emerging from it; they encounter the joy and serenity of conscience, which apart from confession they cannot find elsewhere.

No one, in fact, has the power to free us from our sin, except God. And man who obtains such a remission, receives the grace of a new life of the spirit, which only God, in his infinite goodness, can bestow on him.

The Free Gift of Two Existences

The man and the woman, before becoming man and wife, emerge from the mystery of creation prior to anything else as brother and sister in the same humanity. The comprehension of the nuptial significance of the body in its masculinity and femininity reveals the depth of their freedom, which is the freedom of a gift.

This gives rise to that communion of persons in which both encounter each other and give themselves to each other in the fullness of their subjectivity. Thus, both grow as persons-subjects, and they grow reciprocally, one for the other, through a nakedness free of shame.

If man and woman cease to be reciprocally disinterested gift, as they were for one another in the mystery of creation, they become aware that "they are naked" (cf. Gn 3).

Modesty, the Essential Rule for "Communion of Persons"

In the experience of modesty, the human being knows fear in confrontations with the "second I" (thus, for example, woman in man's presence), and this is substantially fear for one's own "I." Through modesty, the human being almost "instinctively" manifests the need for the affirmation and acceptance of this "I," according to its rightful value. He experiences it at the same time either in himself or outside of himself, before "another." Hence, we can say that modesty is a complex experience even in the sense that, by so to speak putting distance between one human being and another (woman and man?), it seeks at the same time to bring them together personally, creating a base and a suitable level for them.

For the same reason, modesty has a fundamental meaning both for the formation of ethos in human living together and particularly in the man-woman relationship. The analysis of modesty clearly indicates how deeply it is rooted precisely in mutual relationships, how exactly it expresses the essential rules for "communion of persons," and likewise how profoundly it touches the dimension of man's original "solitude."

Thanks to a Baby Without a House There Is a House for Man

The feast of Christmas confirms in a special way the primacy of the family in the life of each of us.

At this time when God is born as man, every man turns to the place where he was born, to those human beings who are his parents: to his father and mother and the children of those parents—his brothers and sisters. Each one finds himself in that basic circle, in that house which he has a right and duty to call his own: the family house.

Precisely on that night when God is born as a baby deprived of a house, all those who turn to that baby with faith and with their heart experience a special nostalgia for their home.

God Comes for Man, for a Communion with Man

If God "comes" to man, he does so because in the human being there is a capacity for expectation and a capacity for welcome such as there is in no other creature. God comes for man, indeed he comes in man, and establishes a very particular communion with him.

Jesus Goes Before Us

"Glory to God in the highest heaven" (Lk 2:14).

God has come near to us. He is in our midst. He is Man. He has been born in Bethlehem. He is lying in a manger because there was no room for him in the inn (Lk 2:7).

His name: Jesus!

His mission: Christ!

He is the messenger of the great counsel, "admirable Counselor" (Is 9:5); and even though two thousand years separate us from his birth, he is always before us and always goes before us. We must "run after him" and "seek to meet him."

He is our peace!

The peace of men!

The peace for those whom he loves (Lk 2:14).

God has become pleased with man through Christ. Man cannot be destroyed; it is not permitted to humiliate him; it is not permitted to hate him!

Christmas, Feast of Man

"Christmas is the feast of man. . . . Man, object of calculation, considered on the basis of the category of quantity . . . and at the same time one, unique, and unrepeatable . . . someone eternally chosen; someone called and summoned by his name" (Christmas Message, 1).

In the face of so many other humanisms, often enclosed in a strictly economic, biological, and psychical vision of man, the Church has the right and the duty to proclaim the truth about man, the truth that she has received from her teacher Jesus Christ. God grant that no external compulsion may impede this. But above all, God grant that she may never cease to do so because of fear and uncertainty, because of letting herself be contaminated by other humanisms, or because of lack of trust in the original message.

DECEMBER 26

Every Christian Is Called to Be a "Good Shepherd"

By reason of baptism every Christian is called to be a "good shepherd" in the circle in which he lives. You parents must carry out the function of the good shepherd toward your children; and you children must also be edifying by your love, by your obedience, and above all by your courageous and solid faith.

Even the mutual relations between spouses must bear the imprint of the example of the good shepherd, so that family life may always be situated at that sublime height of sentiments and ideals willed by the Creator, which has led to the definition of the family as the "domestic Church."

Thus, even in school, at work, in places of sport and leisure activity, in hospitals and places where there is suffering, let everyone seek to be a good shepherd like Jesus.

But above all let those be "good shepherds" in our society who have consecrated themselves to God: religious, sisters, and those who belong to secular institutes.

Only God Can Satisfy the Thirst for Happiness That Overwhelms Man's Heart

Our hearts seek happiness. The Christian knows that genuine fulfillment of this aspiration can be found only in God. Faith assures us that God has come to encounter man in the person of Christ, in whom "dwells all the fullness of the divinity" (Col 2:9).

If man wishes to satisfy the thirst for happiness that overwhelms his heart, it is toward Christ that he must direct his steps. Christ is not far from him.

Our life is one continual succession of encounters with Christ: with Christ present in Scripture, as Word of God; with Christ present in his ministers, as teacher, priest, and shepherd; with Christ present in our neighbor, especially the poor and the outcast who are his suffering members; with Christ present in the sacraments, which are the channels of his saving action; with Christ silent guest of hearts, wherein he dwells and communicates his divine life.

The Supremacy of Love Over Work

It is necessary that man, by his work and the fruits it produces, be able to construct the conditions for his love.

And this supremacy of love in confrontations with work is necessary also for work itself.

Work Must Help Man to Become Better

The riches of the earth, both those that appear on its surface and those that we must seek in the depths of the earth, become the riches of man only at the cost of human work.

This work is necessary—the multiform work of the mind and the hands—so that man may fulfill the magnificent mission that the Creator has entrusted to him, a mission that the book of Genesis expresses in these words: "Subdue it and rule over it" (Gn 1:28). The earth is entrusted to man, and man rules over it by means of work.

Work is also the fundamental dimension of man's existence on the earth. Through man, work has not only a technical meaning but also an ethical one. We can say that man "subdues" the earth when he himself, with his behavior, becomes its lord rather than its slave, and also lord of work rather than its slave.

Work must help man to become better, spiritually more mature and more responsible, so that he can fulfill his vocation on earth, whether as an unrepeatable person, or in community with others, and above all in that fundamental human community that is the family. United to each other, man and woman—precisely in this community whose character has been established by the Creator himself from the very beginning—give life to new men. Work must make it possible for this human community to find the means needed to fashion and preserve itself.

DECEMBER 30

Through Various Paths Men Point to the Same Goal

The paths of men are very different from one another. The immediate objectives that are proposed normally present characteristics that are not only divergent but at times even opposed.

Yet the ultimate goal toward which all instinctively direct themselves is ever the same: all seek personal happiness, within the context of a true communion of love.

If we attempt to penetrate to the most profound of our desires and those of others passing by, we will discover that this is the aspiration common to all. And this is the hope which after failures springs ever anew in the heart of man from the ashes of every delusion.

Toward God

A number does not change only on a calendar. Numbers also change in the life of each one of us: we get older, we advance a little more in this terrestrial journey signaled by individual years; but also by individual months, weeks, and days. Then a question always arises: How are we passing the time that God has assigned us in our earthly journey? What has last year brought, not only in the sphere of material goods (even these have their importance), but as the stage of our journey toward God? These questions are posed.

This evening many men who have social responsibility in the world will hold talks; balances and final totals will be delineated and cheers will be voiced. All of this at the level of human life that is social life, international life, and worldwide life.

But besides this level there exists the level of the individual person, of each of us, in particular of each Christian, who has a special sense of time, of the beginning and the end, because in fact he knows that this time marks the stages of his earthly journey toward God.

† † †

INDEX

(The reference numbers in this index refer to dates)

Advent

is purification 12/2; and progress toward God 12/3; God-man relationship 12/13.

Atheism

enslavement of man 2/7; denial of the Spirit 2/20; and human reality 8/22; denial of freedom 10/13.

Beatitudes

and human reality 2/15, 2/20, 2/22; prerogatives of 4/30, 5/25, 5/26, 5/27.

Beauty

and work 2/6; and greatness of life 2/20; interior 4/13; of nature 8/1, 8/2.

Body

gift of love 2/29, 12/20; nuptial character of 3/29, 8/18; and sensuality 4/12; dignity of 6/2; and modesty 6/16, 6/25, 12/21; significance of 7/24. See also Sexuality.

Catechesis

and Christian virtues 2/15; and popular religiosity 5/29; school of humanity 9/1; and truth 11/11. See also Evangelization.

Charity

virtue of man 1/5; characteristic of bearing witness 1/29; peculiarities of 3/7, 3/8, 3/22, 3/28, 7/23, 9/11; and suffering 5/18; and the Eucharist 7/13, 7/14; voluntary character of 9/17; difficult virtue 9/19. See also Love.

Christ

vocation and exigency for man 1/16; future of history and model of life 1/28, 2/14, 4/26, 7/17; and human solidarity 1/30, 2/12, 4/9, 7/2; makes God known 1/31; teacher 2/14; profound source of truth 2/18, 3/17, 3/26; is not an idea 2/19, 5/23; supreme consolation 2/23; true and eternal priest 2/24; "priest and sacrifice" 3/16; our peace and our joy 4/3, 4/4, 12/24; the meaning of life 6/5, 6/12; bearer of freedom 6/10; does not mortify man 7/7; model of the simple 7/19; and nature 7/19; and children 9/2, 9/3; open the doors to 9/20; easy yoke of 9/22; and mercy 10/8; living bread 10/22; mystery of enlightens man 11/4; came to bring joy 11/14; Master of life 11/14; redeemed us 11/14; gives power of fraternal love 11/16; knowledge of key to understanding world's needs 11/16; union with 12/11.

Christian

first fruit of God's creatures 2/27; priesthood of 4/19; completeness of 7/5; interpreter and guide 7/6; worker for peace 8/5, 8/6; joyous witness 8/13; coherent and courageous witness 8/20; witness of Christ 8/21; who is one 8/24; and temporal tasks 9/24, 9/25; and culture 9/27; eucharistic soul 11/5. See also Witness.

Christmas

God in time 12/17; ray of light 12/18; is the primacy of the family 12/22; communion of God with man 12/23, 12/24; feast of man 12/25.

Church

fidelity to and quest for unity 1/21; and evangelization 1/2, 1/24; contributes to man's development 2/25; relationship of trust with state 2/25; way of man 2/28; and truth 3/17; and integral humanism 3/31; is born from a response of faith 4/2; and culture 4/29, 9/26, 9/27, 11/12; is the truth about man 5/12; as body of Christ 5/20, 8/14; as people of God 5/20, 8/12; and riches 5/28; membership in is a "grace" for every day 6/29; and the state 7/8, 9/16; sanctity of 7/11; and the development of peoples 9/9; and human rights 9/9; and temporal commitments 9/24; and the cross 10/6; missionary character of 10/28; and the prophetic charisma 11/22; mother and bride 12/5; responsible for the Gospel 12/6.

Conscience
measure of man 1/3; and human destiny 1/26; and science 2/10; and human dignity 6/8; criterion for human action 5/31. See also Heart.

Consecration
as gift 2/18; service of love 8/19; coherent and courageous 8/20; and freedom 11/24.

Consumerism
alienation of man 2/8; man cannot be slave to 11/4. See also Materialism.

Conversion
and Eucharist 2/21; as spiritual effort 3/3; openness to God 3/14; ways of 3/24; and justice 5/31; and belief in God 8/10; fruit of prayer 8/28; necessity of 12/1. See also Heart and Grace.

Courage
and witness 1/29, 2/17, 8/20, 9/4; and knowledge 2/10; for a new world 8/23. See also Faith.

Cross
makes God known 1/31; and man's work 2/3; fructifies suffering 3/9; catechesis of 3/10; truth of love 3/11; leaven of charity 3/13; and suffering 3/15; obligatory way to encounter with God 3/16; is always paschal 3/19; beginning of life 4/20; the Christian before 5/30; remembrance, sign, and mystery 10/6.

Culture
way of being human 1/10, 11/30; and Church 4/29, 9/27; there is none opposed to God 9/26; is service to man 10/10, 10/21, 10/24.

Death
and life 3/1, 5/22; and eternal life 11/1, 11/3; and the hope of the living 11/2; part of Easter 11/17. See also Ultimate Realities.

Dialogue

and efficacy of bearing witness 1/21; and unity of Christians 1/22, 4/28; with God in liturgy 2/24; fruit of love 9/29; meaning of 11/21.

Discernment

and the mystery of life 1/27. See also Conscience and Heart.

Egotism

fiction of love 5/9; Christ, solution of 8/31; threat of collective egotism 11/13.

Epiphany

feast of faith 1/2; challenge of God 1/2.

Eucharist

sacrifice of praise 1/27; and Mary 2/13; call to conversion 2/21; and reconciliation 2/21; meeting place of heaven and earth 2/23; memorial of God's love 3/18; realization of the Christian 4/5, 4/19; God in history 4/7; expression of love 5/10; characteristic of the Christian vocation 5/10; and charity 7/13, 7/14, 8/8, 10/12; Sunday, day of 8/30; "word" of Christ 10/14; transforming encounter with Christ 12/10.

Evangelization

mission of the Church 1/2, 5/20; and signs of unity 1/23; and truth 3/17, 11/11; meaning of 5/20, 7/10; and human advancement 11/9. See Witness.

Faith

center of unity 1/21; characteristic of witness 1/29; interior strength of man 2/11; gift of the divine benevolence 2/17, 11/27; basis of human dignity 3/20; reason for joy 4/4; characteristics of 4/11.

Falsehood

and violence 1/17; is against man 6/19. See also Satan.

Family

community of love 5/5, 6/23, 7/9; community of prayer 6/15, 9/12, 9/13; begins with motherhood 6/21; everything depends on it 6/23; man's future 6/23; the Christian family and Sunday 8/30; and Word of God 9/12. See also Matrimony.

Freedom

and truth determine love 4/23, 6/1, 6/2; Christ bringer of 6/10; must be built 6/17; is realized in good and in service 6/20; must be paid for 10/2; comes from God 10/13; man cannot be slave to anything 11/4; and reconciliation 11/10; right to 11/23; donation to God, supreme freedom 11/24; divine law sole standard of 12/12.

Free Time

possibility of praise 8/1; and contemplation 8/2; and rest 8/3; and work 8/3; and suffering 8/4.

Forgiveness

fruit of mercy 3/3; and joy 4/4. See also Mercy.

Fraternity

is constructed "from within" 4/16, 6/16; universal 7/14; and life 7/27; and the Eucharist 8/8, 8/9. See also Solidarity.

God

Word of requires response 1/25; communicates self to us 1/25; known through the universe and through Jesus 1/31; relationship of love to man 1/31; meets man in liturgy 2/24; Lord of time 2/25; makes alliance with man in culture 3/12; man's friend 3/12; man's possibility 4/14; silence of 4/18; attracting power for man 5/16; man's greatness 5/24; man's desire 6/9, 6/18, 10/3, 12/27, 12/31; is truth 6/11; is one family 6/24; is always first 6/28; loves us 6/30, 7/1; foundation of freedom 10/13; man's resurrection 11/16; measure of man 12/4.

Goodness

and truth 1/18; strength of man 4/25; is interior power 6/16; inculcating it is the task of catechesis 9/1.

Gospel

dialogue with man 4/21; power of the Church 4/29; fidelity to 12/12. See also Word of God.

Grace

open to 3/12; possibility of being lost 6/9; and conversion 8/10; and suffering 8/11; source of innocence 8/25; prerequisite for the kingdom 9/2; necessity of 9/18.

Hatred
the world's self-destruction 2/9, 11/13. See also Satan.

Heart
measure of man 1/10, 11/30; as conscience 1/3; hands as landscape of 1/7; the reasons of in creation 6/3; and conversion 8/10, 11/29; source of truth 9/23; conversion of and the unity of Christians 11/29; seeks happiness 12/27, 12/30.

History
and Word of God 3/21.

Holy Spirit
interior fullness 1/3; response to atheism 2/20; love in the divine family 6/24; builds up the church 12/12.

Hope
characteristic of bearing witness 1/29; fruit of contemplation 10/8; does not disappoint 10/25; and desperation 11/15.

Humility
creative submission to truth and love 5/13; and truth 9/2; and abandonment to Christ 9/2.

Interiority
and human formation 1/14, 5/21; and apostolic efficacy 4/10; and nature 8/1, 8/2, 8/25; primacy of 10/1. See also Heart, Conscience, Holy Spirit.

Joy
song, expression of 2/26; fruit of faith 4/4; and suffering 4/6; of the Christian 7/5; importance of 9/28; keynote of Christian message 11/14.

Justice
and love 2/9, 5/3; and social conscience 4/24; and conversion 5/31; united effort of Christians 9/15; and mercy 10/8; foundation of existence 10/10; difficulty of 10/11.

Knowledge (See Science)

Lent
time of light 3/5. See also Conversion.

Liberty (See Freedom)

Life

too brief for love 1/6; dignity and sanctity of 1/16, 2/20, 5/3, 5/4; and culture 1/19; and ultimate realities 1/26; prolongation and completion of the Eucharist 1/27; meaning of 2/25, 6/5, 6/12, 6/13, 7/27, 9/20; and death 3/1, 5/22; journey toward God 4/15; man's proving ground 6/12; proof of fidelity 7/12; sanctity of and unity of Christians 11/29.

Love

of God and man 1/5, 1/6; and will 1/9; and the future 1/10; and science 2/10; characteristics of 2/20, 4/23, 9/10; essence of God's fatherhood 3/4; essential condition of human dignity 5/6, 5/7; and justice 5/8; and humility 5/13; logic of in creation 6/3; and modesty 6/16; and dialogue 9/29; and prayer 9/29; as maturity 10/4; and fear 10/4; as mercy restores man to himself 10/8; and fraternity 11/8; for one another must be hallmark of our lives 11/16; supremacy over work 12/28. See also Charity.

Man

and spiritual interiority 1/3, 2/4; and eternity 1/4; and love 1/4, 5/6, 5/7; and the rights of God 1/8; and knowledge 1/20; must respond to God's Word 1/25; relationship of love to God 1/31; and human realities 2/5; is born of faith 2/11; builds the earth 2/24; meets God in liturgy 2/24; development of 2/25; way of the Church 2/28; growth of 3/12; has God as friend 3/12; and knowledge of God 4/14, 6/9, 6/28, 7/20; personality of 4/12, 12/9; immense reserves of goodness of 5/11; receptacle of every action of God 5/12; value and dignity of 5/17, 6/2, 6/8, 7/16, 9/5, 9/16, 10/16, 10/30, 11/7; the power of 6/4; beginning is in the heart of his mother 6/22; chosen by God 7/1; manager of creation 7/18, 11/18; and mastery of self 7/26; and truth 8/21; voice of creation 8/27; goal of happiness found only in God 10/3; restored to himself by merciful love 10/8; choice of 10/15; cannot be a slave to anything 11/4; cannot eliminate transcendental 11/4; finds light in mystery of Christ 11/4; new man and integral freedom 11/10; hallmark of is love 11/16; forms true community through Christ 11/16; understands world's needs through help of Christ 11/16; limitations of wisdom 12/11; divine law sole standard of his freedom 12/12.

Mary

and the Eucharist 2/13; victory of hope over anguish and death 3/25; window on God 5/14, 5/15; light for man 8/15; and youth 12/8.

Materialism

enslavement of man 2/7, 7/18, 8/22, 10/9, 11/7; and religious freedom 2/7.

Matrimony

partners cannot be self-centered 1/9; or "sexual sharing"? 7/24; value of 7/25, 10/31; and procreation 8/16, 8/17; and love 9/10, 9/12. See also Body, Family, Sexuality.

Matter

reconciliation with 10/3; and contemplation 10/8. See also Materialism.

Mercy

infinite love of God 3/3; and Christ 10/8; most profound source of justice 10/8; restores man to himself 10/8. See also Forgiveness.

Motherhood

woman's vocation 5/2. See also Body, Family, Matrimony, Sexuality.

Nature

and Christ 7/19; and contemplation 8/1, 8/2. See also Beauty, Free Time.

Pardon (See Forgiveness)

Peace

and dialogue 1/1; all men must construct it 2/18, 8/5; threats to 4/22; challenge of 7/3; and consumerism 7/22; fruit of social commitment 9/6; and human progress 9/14; united effort of Christians 9/15; and violence 10/20. See also Dialogue.

Poverty

and riches 2/16, 11/20: and waste 4/17; and human dignity 9/30; and magnanimity 9/30; and underdevelopment 11/19. See also Consumerism, Riches.

Prayer

soul of the world 1/11; and work 1/11, 1/13; and truth 1/12, 6/14; and discernment 1/27; way to conversion 3/24, 6/13, 8/28; climate of ecumenism 4/29; power of God 6/14; and family 6/15, 7/9; and peace 8/6; binding gift 8/29; of Christ, a reason for hope 10/25.

Priest

man of hope 6/6; man of God for his brothers 6/7; celibacy of 6/7, 8/18; missionary of certitude 9/7; and Word of God 11/26; and prayer 11/26; holiness of 11/26.

Reconciliation

and the Eucharist 2/21; and integral liberation 11/10; mercy not condemnation 12/19.

Resurrection

reason for hope and immortality 4/1; and joy 4/4; death and 11/15, 11/17. See also Cross.

Riches

and poverty 2/16, 5/27, 5/28, 11/20; ostentation of 7/31; man cannot be a slave to 11/4. See also Consumerism, Materialism, Poverty.

Sacred Scripture

study of and prayer 11/26. See also Word of God, Gospel.

Sanctity

and life 1/15. See also Conversion, Interiority.

Satan

the evil one, instigator of every snare 8/11; divisive power 8/31.

Science

greatness of man 1/20; true science must be inspired by courage, conscience, and love 2/10; man, manager of 7/4, 11/30.

Sexuality

creative donation 2/29, 7/24, 7/25, 8/16, 8/17; capacity for love 3/29, 12/20; and modesty 6/25, 12/21. See also Body, Matrimony.

Sin
> consciousness of 3/4; waste of humanity 3/30; and conscience 6/27; liberation from 11/10; reality of 12/15.

Solidarity
> with man and with Christ 2/12, 8/7; and the Eucharist 8/9; fruit of social commitment 9/6; first condition of peace 9/14; obligation of 9/21; universal 12/14. See also Fraternity.

Sorrow (See Cross and Suffering)

State
> and Church 7/8, 9/16; service for the community 10/16, 10/18; and human rights 10/16, 10/19; duties of 10/17.

Suffering
> and man's spiritual dimension 1/7; revelation of Christ 1/30; and redemption 2/22; fecundity of 3/6, 3/19, 4/6; mysterious and disconcerting reality 3/23, 3/27; is around us 7/15; spiritual 8/11; paradox of 11/28.

Testimony (See Witness)

Truth
> and peace 1/1; and dialogue 1/1; and communion of spirits 1/1; generates violence if scorned 1/17; and goodness 1/18; and Word of God 2/1; Christ, profound source of 2/18, 3/26; and freedom 4/23, 6/1; and humility 5/13; prophetic power of 6/1; task of the Church 6/2; and science 6/18; and work 6/18; man must live from 6/19; flourishes from the heart 9/23; and evangelization 11/11; right of man 12/16.

Ultimate Realities
> and human consciousness 1/26, 2/5, 4/15, 6/12; and joy 4/4; and the meaning of life 6/12; goal is happiness 10/3; identical goal for all men 10/3.

Unity of Christians
> and bearing witness 1/21; and evangelization 1/21, 1/23, 1/24; and Word of God 8/26; and peace 9/15, 10/26; and justice 9/15.

Vigilance
> task of man 2/5, 2/9.

Violence

is non-truth 1/17; destroys 6/26; and the denial of peace 7/3;
a crime against man 10/20.

Vocation

demand of 1/27; and Word of God 2/2; courage to open oneself to others 9/8; fidelity to 9/23; fruit of faith 10/27.

Will

power of the 6/25; and peace 7/3. See also Conscience,
Heart.

Witness

and unity of Christians 1/21; to Christ 1/22, 5/19, 8/23, 10/
6; faith, hope, and love, characteristics of 1/29; to truth 3/17,
6/11, 11/25; way to liberation 4/1; of joy 4/4, 8/13; demands
of 4/8; youthful 4/27; even to martyrdom 10/5; of the
Church of silence 10/7; and the Eucharist 10/21. See also
Christian, Evangelization.

Word of God

requires response 1/25; foundation of certitude 2/1; man in
confrontation with 2/2, 10/23; immutable in time 3/21; and
unity of Christians 8/26; and witness 9/4; bread that we
need 9/18; and human words 9/18. See also Sacred Scripture,
Gospel.

Work

and prayer 1/11, 1/13; and the cross, 2/3; and beauty 2/6;
service to mankind 5/1, 11/6; fundamental dimension of life
7/20; nobility of 7/28, 9/2; Christian conception of 7/29, 11/
6; and justice 7/30, 10/11; and free time 8/3; and human maturity 12/29.

Youth

and witness 4/27; the magic of 8/31; and charity 9/17; and
the value of life 12/7; and Mary 12/8.

BIBLIOGRAPHICAL NOTE

(At the end of Index in the Italian)

A great many of the passages of John Paul II have been selected by us from the *Osservatore Romano*. However, we are in part indebted to the anthology made by Edizioni Paoline entitled *Il Papa Ci Parla* [*The Pope Speaks to Us*], which contains the best of the Pontifical Magisterium, and to the series of booklets by Edizioni O. R. of Milan, especially for the encyclical *Redemptor hominis* [*The Redeemer of Man*] and the Magisterium in Brazil.

We have also made good use of our publication *Parole di Certezza* [*Word of Certitude*] and the books published by the Vatican Press: *La Bottega dell'Orefice* [*The Goldsmith's Shop*], *Il Sapore del Pane* [*The Taste of Bread*], and *Pietra di Luce* [*Stone of Light*].

For several days, new passages have been substituted for the original edition. These include the selections for January 9, from the Pope's Mass at Limerick, Ireland; January 25, from a talk in West Germany on Nov. 18, 1980; January 31, from the encyclical *Rich in Mercy*, #2; for February 24, from a talk to the College of Cardinals, June 28, 1980; for February 25, from address to politicians in West Germany, Nov. 15, 1980; March 12, homily in the Cathedral of Rio de Janeiro, July 2, 1980; October 3, from speech in Fortalea, Brazil, July 9, 1980; October 8, from the encyclical *Rich in Mercy* #14; November 4, from speech in Brazil, June 30, 1980; November 14, from talk in Harlem, New York City, Oct. 2, 1979; November 16, from the homily at Shea Stadium, New York, Oct. 3, 1979; December 11, from seminary address in Philadelphia, Oct. 4, 1979; and December 12, from address at Logan Airport, Philadelphia, Oct. 3, 1979.